UNFORGETTABLE

MW00442000

THE SECOND MY LIFE CHANGED FOREVER

Eileen Doyon

The Second My Life Changed Forever

Published by October Hill, LLC
www.unforgettablefacesandstories.com

Layout and cover design by
Kirsten Larsen Schultz | LarsenEdge Marketing Solutions
www.larsenedge.com

Printed in the United States of America.

ISBN: 0692709118
ISBN-13: 978-0692709115

Thank You

I would like to personally say "Thank You" to everyone that has supported me from day one of Unforgettable Faces and Stories. Whether you follow Unforgettable Faces & Stories on our website, Facebook, Twitter, LinkedIn, YouTube or are on our email list, "Thank You". For all of you that have purchased any one of my books, told a friend, sent a referral, sent me a note, and most importantly, give me support, "Thank You." For without all of you, I would not be where I am today! "Thank You."

And thank you for purchasing The Second My Life Changed Forever! We are very excited about this sixth book in the Unforgettable Faces & Stories series.

Other books in the Unforgettable Faces & Stories series:
Dedications: Dads & Daughters
Keepsakes: Treasures from the Heart
Best Friends: Forever & Ever
Pet Tales: Unconditional Love
Letters To Heaven

As we grow our community of storytellers, we'd appreciate your help in getting the word out about us. Here are a few ways you can help:
* Like / share our Facebook page: www.facebook.com/unforgettablefacesandstories
* Connect with Eileen on Linked in: www.linkedin.com/in/eileendoyon
* Review our books on Amazon
* Send us a video testimonial. See sample testimonials on our website: www.unforgettablefacesandstories.com/videos or on our YouTube channel www.youtube.com/user/FacesandStories.
* We love written testimonials too!

Thank you again for your support! We would love for you to participate in one of our upcoming books…YOUR story told by YOU!

ꟾNTRO

The hands on a clock tick away....tic toc...tic toc...tic toc.....In one of those seconds.....our entire life can change forever, positive or negative. We have our plans all in place, we've written it all out and are moving right along and sometimes better and faster than planned....and then it happens......the hands on the clock are going tic toc...tic toc...tic toc...and wham....a second goes by and then it happens.......that one second that changes our life forever..... Sometimes we wish we could go back and smash that clock, but we cannot. Life goes on after that second happens.

In "The Second My Life Changed Forever", you will be able to read how these people handled that second in time, whether it was positive or negative, and moved forward in time in minutes, hours, days, and even years. As you read about their second, think about your own life and how things could change in a second for you........

Unforgettable Faces & Stories

The Second My Life Changed Forever

ALLIE SILVERNALE

Saturday, June 4th, 2011
Walmart Parking Lot in Princeton, Indiana
I was 24
I met my future husband

I never wanted to get married, I never wanted children. I had one goal and that was to be a career driven woman who was not dependent on anyone. I will never know why I decided to go to Walmart that morning. From the moment I got out of my car and saw him standing there smiling at me in the Walmart parking lot at 7:30 am that Saturday morning, my life was forever changed.
I flew home that weekend from Charlotte, NC to go to a wedding. I thought I had planned it perfectly. Fly into St. Louis, get in and out of Mt. Carmel as quickly as possible. I got home in time for the rehearsal dinner, went straight to Evansville, stayed the night at a friends, then headed home that Saturday morning to take a nap, shower, and get ready to go to the wedding.   I then had to leave at 3am to make my 5am flight from St. Louis back to Charlotte Sunday morning. The perfect plan. In and out of Mt. Carmel before running into anyone, right? Wrong!

For some reason at 7:30am that Saturday morning, when I was making my way back to Mt. Carmel to nap and get ready, I decided at the last minute to make a nascar turn into Walmart to go pick up some DVD's to record the wedding on. The whole time I was driving up to park my car I was cursing myself asking why in the world I was going to Walmart so early? I could easily stop by there on my way to Evansville for the wedding. For some reason I didn't turn around to head home. I parked my car still cursing myself saying I was losing out on some valuable "nap time". As I am getting out of the car, I noticed someone was staring at me, the sun was shining so bright I could barely see, but then all of a sudden I got a good look at the man who was "checking me out" (as he quotes when he tells the story), and I said "Oh my gosh! I haven't seen you forever!" It was him, smiling so big at me, not even realizing who I was just yet till I laughed. We laughed, hugged, went shopping around Walmart together, and he was telling me all about all the major changes in his life. I could see he had changed so much since I knew him in high school. Something was so different about him. He was so excited when he started telling me about the house he was renting, and had plans to buy it and fix it up. He was so proud and he had to show me. So we headed back to town and I met him at his house. It was a DUMP (I say that nicely, lol). But he was so proud because he knew what he could do with it. We had so much fun sitting outside talking about everything that had changed since the last time we saw each other. I didn't even realize 4 to 5 hours went by and it was time for me to get ready and head to the wedding. I was actually running SO LATE. Needless to say, he was suppose to work that night, but decided to call in and hang out with me. After the wedding, I came home and he picked me up and we hung out with friends around the campfire till 3am when I had to leave. I had so much fun. I didn't understand why I couldn't stop smiling. No guy had ever made me feel that way after just hanging out for one night. So I tried to brush it off. I didn't want to give it to much thought. But, he had different plans. He texted me that next morning and every morning from there on out. I never went without a "Good morning beautiful" text when he got off work the next morning. He made me smile every morning, and I finally couldn't take it anymore. A couple weeks in, I decided to finally ask him what he was thinking? Because I knew my feelings were growing stronger day by day and I knew falling for him meant I would be moving home. I was in love with Charlotte, NC, and wanted to stay there. God had different plans, because when I texted him to ask him what he was thinking, his response was (& I quote) "You're sexy, smart, fun, good-looking in my arms, and put on this earth for me. And that house is awful big for just me."

After that, in a nutshell, I moved home to move in with him Thanksgiving weekend of 2011 (that same year), we were engaged by March 2012, married by September 22, 2012, bought our new home December 2012 (life happened he wasn't physically able to build a home anymore without worrying his wife to death), and then we were blessed with the most amazing gift of our lives, our son on August 5th, 2014. I still have my career, but I found my true purpose of my life that Saturday, June 4th, 2011, and that was to build an amazing life that I never knew I wanted with my partner and best friend. Best. Decision. Ever. Everything I had ever thought I wanted, no longer mattered, and everything I never knew I always wanted is now my whole world. So I learned, you have no idea what you really want in life, and sometimes the biggest risks and leaps of faith are the best decisions ever. Whatever you want to call it, "serendipity" or an "act of God" some things are meant to be if you just listen to your gut and take that terrifying leap. Life is amazing.

I have an amazing life. Yes, there are hard times, but I have my partner by my side, and we get through it - together as a team. And we created an amazing little boy who I never would have thought I could love so much. I want the simple life now because as long as I have my family, that is all that matters.

ANGELA FRY

When we contemplate instances that have shaped our lives, I wonder how often it actually is that we realize in that split second that our lives have changed forever. I would imagine that in most cases, it is days or months or maybe even years later that we realize the affect; if we realize at all. The second my life changed forever occurred on 24 May 2010, in the deserts of Iraq. That split second tumbled me into years of what I can only refer to as survivor's guilt. That tailspin affected not only my career, but also relevant family and fraternal relationships.

I guess it is now that I will deal with the issue in the same manner I deal with most of life's issues: through the written word. I hope you enjoy my short story of survival and sacrifice and my realization that although our lives are intertwined, one person's survival does not have to occur at the sacrifice of someone else. When we have the opportunity to speak with those who have survived harrowing circumstances, rarely do we say or hear, "I survived because I'm a badass." We are most likely to hear something like, "But for the grace of God go I," or "I guess I was the lucky one."

Sometimes we may even elaborate on rituals of preparation for missions, such as lucky charms or regularly-stated prayers that we attribute as our reason for survival. Perhaps it is merely superstition or perhaps our need for rituals that gift us with some psychological advantage as we face the unknown. Perhaps that ritual includes the possession of something as simple as a St. Christopher medallion, or a photo, or a letter from home. Regardless, it is quite often that Soldiers have recited stories that explain their reason for survival, which often leads to severe issues of survival guilt as they remember those who were not lucky enough to return.

Christmas 2015, a friend gave me the book, The Lucky One. She explained that as she read the book, she could not help but think of me and hoped the book might help me get through the holiday season. "Maybe the book will help you deal with the issues that you ignore for yourself and help everyone else deal with," she expressed.

The underlying story of the book is a Marine who survived three combat tours to Iraq. Many of his comrades give credit of his survival to a photo he came across during one of his tours; a possession that could be considered either a blessing or a curse, depending on the outcome of his journey. I must admit that early into the book, I understood why she thought of me as she continued to read. Initially, the book did not help. Instead, it seemed to set me back as I progressed through this holiday season. As I continued to read, I could not help but remember my own story of survival and sacrifice and realized that life goes on and our memories make us who we are.

After hours of complaining about leaving COB Adder for Victory Base Complex, I asked my friend and mentor, Maj. Culver, "What time is it, Sir?" He understood my hesitancy to return to brigade headquarters, far away from the Cavalry Squadron. He looked at me and with an exaggerated effort spit his tobacco into his makeshift spittoon. In his southern twang, he said, "Small Fry, you ain't got a watch?"

As I shook my head no, he looked down at his wrist and removed his rather worn G-Shock. He walked around his desk, knelt down in front of me and buckled his old watch to my wrist. "I have worn this watch on every combat mission I have ever been on," he gently said.

I shot up from my seat and stated that I could not take his watch, as I was more than painfully aware of the dozens of funerals he had attended during his military career. He placed his hands on my shoulders and guided me back down into my seat and continued, "We lost Troops but I never took this watch off and I made it home without a scratch. You wear this watch...never take it off and you will make it home to your family and back to the Cav safe and sound."
I accepted the watch and made the long trek to Baghdad, begrudgingly, as for some reason I felt more at home with the gung-ho Troops of the 2-108th Cavalry Squadron. I enjoyed the greeting of the day: "Sound the Charge, ma'am," and loved hearing formations end with, "If you ain't Cav, you ain't shit!"

A few hours after arriving in Baghdad, I was greeted with a source of annoyance, as every evening at exactly 1800, the watch alarm would go off. I called that evening from VBC and asked, "How the heck do I turn the alarm off?" He laughed, "I ain't telling you because every day at 1800, when that alarm goes off you will think about the squadron and that you need to get your butt back down here with your Troopers."

Less than a month later, after Maj. Culver jokingly promised to send the Cavalry to rescue me from the evil brigade, I did return to Adder. A few days after my arrival, I sent Maj. Culver and the convoy escort team from Bravo Company off on a security mission only to be jolted from my bed at 0323 on 24 May 2010, with news that he had been killed in an IED explosion.

To this day, there are no words to express the sense of loss the entire squadron felt with his death. With the chaotic events of the day, the gift of his watch and all that it entailed had not crossed my mind. As I returned to my office after attempting to force myself to eat, the alarm on Maj. Culver's G-Shock chimed at exactly 1800, as I walked across COB Adder. It was at that exact second that I realized he had gone on his first combat mission without his lucky watch. I stood there…alone…breathing the dusty Iraq air….as his family, friends and Troopers mourned the loss of a hero.

ANNA WILLIAMS

April 2009
My dad's office
8 years old

My dad showed me a short news clip of a teenage boy somewhere in the US making a pen on a lathe. The boy turned his pen-making hobby into a small business. My dad thought it was a great example of how even kids can do big things if they choose to.

When I finished watching that video, I told my dad that I wanted to start my own business making pens. He kind of laughed and said no. I was mad and asked if it was because I was a girl. He told me it was because I was 8 years old and I could get seriously hurt trying to use a lathe.

I can't explain why, but I couldn't let it go. A few months would go by and I would ask again. Always with the same response. I turned 9 and asked again. Still a great big NO. Finally, I turned 10 and said to my dad, "Dude, double digits, can I make pens now?" For the first time he hesitated, then said "maybe". I could hardly contain myself. I remember pleading with my dad to take me to the store right then to buy me a lathe. The next day, we went to Harbor Freight and bought my first lathe. We brought it home and I didn't even give my dad a chance to read the instructions. I know he was getting irritated with me because I wasn't being patient. I told him I knew what I was doing. For some reason it just all made sense to me. Over the next 2 weeks I was out in the garage every day after school making pens. I think it was the fourth or fifth pen that I took to my dad and he was very surprised at how well I did.

One day my neighbor came over and asked if he could watch me make a pen from start to finish. I asked him if he had any plans because it would take me about 2 hours. He stayed and watched the whole process. When I was done, I gave him the pen. He just kept staring at it and then asked me if I could make 15 more just like it. I thought he was kidding. He owned a small business and wanted to give them to his clients.

We have friends and family around the US so my dad thought it would be cool to create a free website just to share some pictures of the pens I was making instead of sending them in emails. He also suggested that I come up with a business name. I decided on Pens Ink because I liked the play on words. So my dad ordered me some inexpensive business cards and setup my Pens Ink website. My website was only 2 pages. The first page was just a bunch of pen pictures and the second page was a "contact" page so people could send me an encouraging message. One day I came home from school and had an inquiry from Australia asking if they could buy a pen from me. After a few emails, I closed the sale. I ran to my neighbor's house to tell them that I just got an order from Australia. I went on to say that I didn't know where that was, but I knew it was far away.

After my first international sale at 10 years old, my dad explained the importance of running my business the right way and I needed to setup a DBA and start paying taxes.

At 15, I'm starting my 6th year in business and continue to grow. Little did I know that a 2 minute video would change my life in a way that I could never have comprehended at 8 years old.

You can have a million people believing in you, but it won't matter if you don't believe in yourself. As a young entrepreneur, you need a lot of support. For me, I had my dad. If your support can't come from your parents then find it somewhere else. Maybe it's a teacher, coach, grandparents, or a best friend. These are the people that can help you stay focused, and guide you.

Owning my own business has taught me that anything is possible if you put your mind to it. Following a passion isn't easy but it can be very rewarding. The money is nice, but it's much more than that. I am so much more aware of how I have an ethical responsibility to my customers and my community.

I would love nothing more than to build a business that offers jobs to people. To build a business that treats its employees well and gives back to the community. I want to know that I did something good with what I created.

ANNMARIE ALBISTON

May 2005
Maine Medical Center, Portland, Maine
I was 43 years old

The phone rang in the early morning hours. It was my mother saying something was wrong with my father and she had called 911. We all made it to the hospital in record time! My father had had a massive stroke. There were many unknowns in the early stages of dad's stroke. Would he walk? Would he drive? Would he talk? What would his quality of life be like? I knew dad was a fighter, but I also knew that a stroke wasn't good.

In the blink of an eye, my father's happy, productive, and fun life changed drastically, and so did ours! A week in the hospital, then several weeks in rehab was hard work for dad, but he was determined. I was by his side from morning until night. I swabbed his mouth, helped him eat, encouraged and supported him, and went to all of his therapies with him. When dad was tucked in for the night, I would go home and my husband had a hot meal waiting for me. We had a little bit of time for conversation, then to bed and to do it all over again the next day.

During speech therapy one day, the therapist said that dad had Aphasia. I remember thinking, dad had a stroke, what is aphasia? I had much to learn! Aphasia is a communication disorder. One out of four stroke patients can end up with Aphasia. In simple terms, Aphasia is Loss of Language, Not Intellect. Imagine knowing what you want to say, but not being able to get the words out. Frustrating, you bet!

Dad needed a considerable amount of care when he went home, and he still had outpatient therapy during the week. Every day I would travel the 30 minutes to my parents' home, take him to his therapies, take him home, and then travel back to our home. I ran errands, did their grocery shopping, cooked....the list is long. I loved every second of being with my father, but it was exhausting! Life as I knew it had changed considerably! My father's health and well being became a priority in my life. I spent huge amounts of my time with my father and my mother every day. My husband never complained! Our life now focused on taking care of my father, and my mother too!

It soon became necessary for my parents to move in with us. We finished off some space and made a beautiful in law apartment. No more back and forth; my parents were now just across the porch from us. Having them with us made some things easier and some things more difficult. It was difficult to watch my father become isolated by friends and family. He was still the same wonderful man, but because he couldn't communicate like he once could, people stopped calling and stopping by. It was so sad to watch.

We worked hard to give my father the best quality of life possible. He loved being around people, loved to laugh - he loved life.

With little to no local support for folks with Aphasia, we knew we had to do something. My dad needed support so we knew many others did too! One summer we literally stumbled upon the Adler Aphasia Center in New Jersey and the wheels started turning! We toured the center and watched folks with Aphasia having fun, laughing, engaging in conversation, doing arts and crafts, smiling, being creative – they were out of the house and they were doing something that made them feel good! How my father would love it! We needed an Aphasia Center in Maine; we needed to help people with aphasia!

How do we start an Aphasia Center? Who will come? The questions were many! We partnered with two organizations and organized a weekend retreat for folks with Aphasia and their families/friends. Our first retreat welcomed 11 folks with aphasia, and we had 24 folks with aphasia at our last retreat. With families, friends and volunteers, 90 people took part in our 4th retreat! In 2016, we will have our 5th Annual Andre R. Hemond Aphasia Retreat Weekend. Due to the challenges my father endured after his stroke, and being his caregiver, it led us to help many other folks who have Aphasia and their families/friends. We have gone a step further with the new creation of the Adaptive Outdoor Education Center. It is a lodge where folks with any disability may stay for a minimum cost. There is much good that can come from a sad and difficult situation. Patience, love, humor, support, empathy, and hugs are all a big part of working with people who have varying abilities.

My husband and I have formed a non profit – the Albiston Foundation. It is two-fold: 1. The Aphasia Center of Maine and 2. The Adaptive Outdoor Education Center   We work tirelessly to provide quality of life programs for people of all abilities. Our family has grown to include the people who attend our retreats and the people we meet on a daily basis. I feel very blessed and my heart is filled with compassion and love. My father would love what we are doing and I know he is very happy and proud that his name is on the retreat we do for folks with Aphasia. He was an educator his entire life, and through the Andre R. Hemond Aphasia Retreat weekend, outreach, and more, he continues to educate!

My life changed in a second, for sure! Caring and being there for my father every step of the way is a gift I will always cherish. How fortunate I was to have the unwavering support and love from my husband while I spent hours away from him each day. We put our lives on hold to give my father what he needed – love, comfort, compassion, care, and so much more!

I watched my father take his last breath six years after his massive stroke. His was a life well lived. Although the challenges were many for my dad, how blessed I was to be able to learn, grow, share, and love even more! I wish dad never had the stroke, yet if it weren't for my father having the stroke, we wouldn't be doing what we are doing now. He would be happy to know that good things have come.

Annemarie
Aphasia Website: www.aphasiacenterofmaine.org
Adaptive Outdoor Education Center: www.adaptiveoutdooreducation.org

BARRY MOORE

November-2011
Albany, New York

I started a new company after retiring from my career. This improved my self being and changed my life forever. The lessons I learned were motivation and drive does matter! This has shaped my life in that I have done things that I would have never done.

In late 2011 after I retired from my Postal Career, my son and I started JNB Foods. We had our first production in the spring of 2012. At first, our thought process was to be a farmer's market food company. This meaning that we would only do farmers' market retailing. Early in our start-up, we decided to test our products at a womens' expo in Albany, New York. After two full days, we sold out our entire first production, and with that said, I was approached by the lead dietitian of a grocery store chain in the Albany area. Within months, we were in 35 ShopRite grocery stores! After the contract with the grocery stores, we were well received in several other markets such as specialty food stores, wineries, and health food stores, gift shops, and more!

We look for events each week to help us brand our company. Some of the events we have done to date are fund raisers to help community events for its citizens. We do several events with the Taste of New York coordinated through the Department of Agriculture and Markets. We participated in the Summer Fancy Food show in New York City. We have done events in several wineries and supported other local functions such as Cinco de Mayo in the City of Albany. Being a Navy Veteran, I also work with the Veterans Outreach Center and the Small Business Administration in the co-ordination of events and other ventures to support our Veteran Families.

We have grown every year since and have now begun the process of international trade with China and are looking to the future of other countries to ship our products to. Our goal here is to help expand into the Western food markets in Asia and other parts of the world.

Barry Moore
JNB Foods

WWW.JNBFOODS.COM
On Facebook: jnbfoods1
On Twitter @jnbfoods

BRITTANY BIVONA

What a Hero brings back is a story: This is my story. Everybody is the hero of their own lives. In Buddhism, we must win every day and overcome our obstacles and struggles.

That moment my life changed forever and took a huge turn to lead me on the right path doing my human revolution is when I was first introduced to Nichirien Buddhism by my client. Why I chose this as the moment that changed my life, because if you ever knew what I was like four years ago, I have completely transformed myself with my Buddhist practice. IT HAS CHANGED MY LIFE FOREVER!!!!

I have been practicing Nichiren Buddhism for the past three years. My Buddhist practice helped transform me to the best that I can be at whatever I do by recognizing that I am a Buddha with unlimited self-esteem and unlocking my potential through the power of chanting Nam Myoho Renge Kyo. Nam Myoho Renge Kyo means devotion to the mystic law through cause and effect and vibration; you're literally aligning yourself with the universe with the mini universe that lies within you. All living beings has the essence of Nam Myoho Renge kyo, everybody is a Buddha even when they don't even know it. My personality remained the same but as I continue to struggle and win, I gain more confidence and became more courageous and compassionate towards myself and others. My Buddhist practice and working for happiness of others is what changed my life forever.

What if someone told you that you have the power to do anything, it seems a little unrealistic. Do we really have the power to do anything? Well, YES absolutely!!! You have to be true to yourself and tap into unlocking your potential. Be fearless, have courage, and conquer the dragon. What if someone told you about the power of being HAPPY right now? The struggles I went through my whole life is what made me who I am today. I love to help others and inspire others, but we also help and inspire each other along the way in our heroic journey.

How everything happens for a reason. You hear it all the time when something doesn't go right or you didn't get the job you wanted, someone tells you these words of wisdom- "don't worry, everything happens for a reason." You feel better because you know they're right. My mom would be the one to tell me this when I was going through major panic attacks. I believed her but at the same time I didn't feel like everything happens for a reason. I was easily discouraged and my negative thoughts would take over and always thought I was full of bad luck. I was very insecure and doubting myself all the time. I wasn't always like this. There were days I felt like I can take on the world because I always enjoyed everything I was doing. My life changed when I moved to New Hampshire three years ago. It wasn't that simple yet. I didn't just move here and 'whala' and I am a new and transformed person, confident and happy. Nope, it wasn't that easy and I had to take a lot of action. It wasn't until now that the struggles I faced during my whole life, especially in the past three years are what made me who I am today. These struggles helped with my transformation process. Every day I continue to struggle. I further improve myself to get better, gain more wisdom, learn from my mistakes, and become more confident. Oh and it gets better. I smile and I am the happiest while I face adversity.

Throughout my journey since then, I found out that nobody can make me feel bad about myself. I can't blame anybody for making me feel insecure or unhappy. I take full responsibility in how I felt during my dark times. Since 2012, I had many struggles and for the past year and half I have been on a weight loss/fitness journey. I always loved spinning classes since 2009, but when I took spin classes at Lizfit, I was hooked and addicted. I decided to become a spinning instructor inspired by many people especially Liz Forkel. I love to work out and I especially love spinning classes- nothing better than being on bike with good tunes and especially cycling to the beat. I thought to myself if I was able to teach spin classes, I can help other people get healthy and fit and be happy. It strongly relates to my Buddhist practice like everything else that I do but this would be my human revolution. In my Buddhist practice and being part of the Soka Gakkai, which is an amazing peace organization that spreads peace, culture, and education all over world through studying Buddhist teachings, everything that we do (achieving our goals) we do it for kosen rufu- world peace. And this is a ripple effect as we share our experiences and encourage one another by encouraging each other to never give up, never be defeated, and always have faith because we can win at anything. When I shared my experience last year after I started co-teaching with my mentor, Liz, it felt good to inspire and encourage everyone. I got over my fear of public speaking, being up on a bike while everyone stares at you waiting for you to tell them what to do is rather intimidating. I also had to make the work out fun and engaging and challenging.

TRANSFORMATION

I have been on my weight loss journey for the past year and half and I met another amazing woman, Liz Forkel, who I resonate with profoundly. Again, I felt like I knew her before physically meeting her. It all starts with diet and exercise to really win in life and achieve your personal goals, career goals, and fitness goals. I became a Beachbody coach and love to help others to eat healthy and take control over their eating habits with eating a balanced diet and portion control. I continue to struggle but this time I reduced the intensity and frequent amount of panic attacks and most importantly, I am happy. I smile at the face of adversity. Because of my struggles, I have more faith in myself. "On Every heroic journey, faith is challenged." So the more we struggle, our faith is being challenged because then we become stronger, build more confidence, character, and faith. In Buddhism, we call this the 10 demon daughters (you can visualize them anyway you like but it's nothing negative about it), they are there for your protection to stay strong and to continuing having faith in yourself.

Stay Focus: I know exactly what I want and envision myself doing all the things I love to do and making a living. I realized if I am doing too many things at once or I am in two places at once (not physically possible, but mentally it is and it's distracting) it is like chasing my own tail, if I had one. Focus on one thing at a time and eventually everything will be integrated. Make a list of goals, take action, make it happen, and check it off. And have faith in yourself, smile and be happy!!!! Life is a journey; it's all about the experience. The Hero brings back a story, so make the best experience every time and write your story.

CARRIE GENDREAU

It was in June 2001 that I stepped into my Optometrist's office for what I thought was going to be a routine pre-approval for Lasik surgery.

After spending quite a bit of time examining my eyes, my eye doctor looked at me and said "I cannot approve this surgery. You have what appears to be a tumor in your left eye. I am not sure, but it could be Primary Acquired Melanosis."

He immediately referred me to an ophthalmologist. My visit involved with the ophthalmologist required more examination. My ophthalmologist said that it does appear to be a tumor and wanted to see if it was growing. He took a biopsy of the tumor. Sure enough the tumor was growing and it proved to be malignant. My ophthalmologist operated on the tumor and removed it. He did indicate if it grew back he was going to refer me to Mass Ear and Eye Infirmary in Boston.

During this time I never really grasped the seriousness of what was going on.

The tumor did grow back and I was off to Boston. My eye doctor in Boston said that she would operate and remove this second tumor. She also indicated that this is nothing to mess with and she had patients dying from this very thing.

It was at this point, I realized the seriousness of what I was dealing with. I wrote out my obituary and funeral arrangements. I wanted to get my affairs in order. My daughter, Emmalee, was 11 years old. I wrote out scripts to produce on DVDs for her to pop in at different stages of her life. Scripts that said "Hi Emm this is Mom….Happy 16th Birthday, Hi Emm, this is Mom….. Happy Graduation, Hi Emm, sure wish I could be there for this special day of your wedding…, etc.

I was still working full time and working on my Master's Degree. I shared with the group that I was training that I had eye cancer. One of the guys in the group painted a picture for me. He said that once I went blind I could still feel the picture and see what was there. This painting hangs in my office, even today, as a reminder of God's goodness.

There was some deep soul searching. There were many people praying for my healing. I grew up in a Christian home and we always prayed. My Mom asked me if I would ever consider a "healing service". I hadn't. I thought of the healing services as a bit hokey.

I contacted my Pastor about what a healing service would look like. I didn't want to make a mockery of my Lord and Savior. My Pastor shared with me that in his 28 years of ministry no one had ever asked for a healing service. For a few weeks I searched Scripture and asked God to show me what His Will was for me? At some point during those few weeks, I realized that whether I was healed here on earth or God took me Home, I was going to be healed. This was one of the most gut wrenching times of my life. I HAD to surrender.

Running parallel with this is my Mom asking God for a sign that I was going to be healed. An answer to that prayer was about to unfold. One evening my Mom and Dad were on their 200 acres of land enjoying a cup of coffee and 4 deer show up—first of all deer don't just "show up". My Dad grabs the camera and starts taking pictures. The deer led him up a trail. They stop. The deer head back down toward Mom. Dad now explains that the deer appeared to "be looking for someone or something". The deer stop facing Mom, and then one by one three of them walk by my Mom on her left side and stop. The fourth deer hesitated. After just a few moments the fourth deer walks up to Mom on her right side and stops. The next morning Mom awakes and realizes this WAS her sign. The first three deer represent the Father, Son, and Holy Spirit and the fourth deer represented me. It was if the Lord was saying-- "Carrie is going to be just fine."

In the meantime I am back in Boston. The third tumor is aggressively growing. My eye surgeon also found 3 malignant tumors in my right eye. She said that she wanted to start me on topical chemo starting in October of 2002. I asked her if I could have until November.

I decided to go ahead with a healing service. My Pastor, two Deacons, my Mom and Dad, my daughter and husband all gathered in a small Sunday-School room for prayer. The Pastor anointed my head with oil and prayed. There wasn't anything unusual that happened. Everyone one in the room however felt the presence of God.

Fast forward to November 2002—a month later. My husband and I are sitting in Dr. Colby's exam room in Boston. Her assistant comes in and examines my eyes. He doesn't say a word. He goes from my eyes and to my chart. This happened several times. He finally said "Dr. Colby will be with you in a few minutes."

Dr. Colby comes in and does her usual routine. She goes to the sink, washes her hands and asks if there are any changes in my health. I said "I sure do hope so". She then sat down on her stool and began to examine my eyes. She kept going back to the chart and to my eyes. She did this several times. She finally pushed back on her stool and took off her readers. She said "Carrie, I don't know what to tell you. Not only is the third tumor gone, the scar tissue is healed and the three tumors in your right eye are completely gone."

I shared with her about the healing power of God. She then said "Well, I did have a patient get struck by lightening once and was healed".

Even in spite of the evidence, I still had to go back for follow-up visits. Finally after a couple of years, I told Dr. Colby that I was going to die, but it would NOT be from eye cancer.

God IS the Great Physician.

CHRISTINE BUYCE

February 1990

I was in Holland for the second semester of my sophomore year of college, living in a castle. Yes, a castle. Even better, four day class weeks allowed an extra day to travel, love Europe! I was away from the city life of Boston. This small village felt like home. It is in the asparagus region of Holland and has two lane country roads.

It was on one of those first long weekend trips that we chose Rome. It took a bus and a twenty-four hour train to get there. I remember talking about my father nonstop. We had time.

I remember one particular stop on the train, in Switzerland. It was the middle of the night and we poked our heads out of the train knowing we may never get a chance to see the Alps again. It was dark and I remember looking up and seeing the Big Dipper. The same one I see from the deck at home sitting out with my dad when he gets home from the 7 to 11 shift at the paper mill.

I looked up and thought of him without knowing that on this day he decided to take his own life. He was alive to me and dead to my family. I got back on the train still talking about my dad as some of them had met him at parents' weekend and enjoyed my funny stories.

We found Rome to be fast paced and we did a lot in a very short amount of time including the Ruins, Vatican, and The Spanish Steps. We decided the journey back was long and headed out a day early. There were no cell phones or computers at this time to tell me what had happened. My dad was still alive to me.

We arrived exhausted at the castle, having to walk a ways from the bus stop. My close friend was the first to see us. She looked angry with us. I now realize it was shock. She did not expect to see us, especially me a day early when all they were thinking about for days was how to tell me, when to tell me, and how to find me to tell me (staying at random youth hostels, no real plan or Internet). They had to wait until we returned. However, everything planned was not for this moment. I headed to my room up the large beautiful wide wooden staircase that the castle has to offer, just past the piano room. I admired that room each time I passed it. I lived in a castle and was grateful for its grandeur. The staircase had a landing as it slowly curved up to my floor. It housed a wooden phone booth where I had spoken to my dad days before. International calls were very expensive limited to once a week or so. Letters were still all the rage. I still have his letters to me.

I got to my room and we were starting to get ready for dinner. The married couple in charge of students appeared at our door. "Who died?" was my first thought as they asked for me. I had four grandparents and I figured it was one of them, but they did not tell me anything. I followed behind them up the back winding staircase, inside the castle walls, to their private quarters. I was in a trance like state at that point trying to figure out who had passed.

They had my brother on the phone when I sat down. I remember him saying that our dad had a heart attack while mowing the lawn. It was February, but maybe he said shoveling, it was a blur as it moved to discussions of me coming home for the funeral. My life changed in that moment, but it had already happened that night on the train.

I was given the gift of having him days longer than my family and not knowing he chose to leave. I was given time in a beautiful place and looking up at the stars in the Swiss Alps as he passed. The castle had a moat with a bridge that my six foot windows overlooked. The grounds hosted weddings due to their beauty. That was my window view. My mother's kitchen window view overlooked the wooded lot where it happened.

I arrived home after a twelve hour plane ride and four hour car ride, still not knowing the truth. My brother approached me at the end of the driveway. At the moment he started to tell me I said, "I already know." He asked "How?" "I just do", I replied.

My life from then on was continuing college in Holland, Boston, and Los Angeles. I was not able to grieve, but had to live for my mom by finishing everything for which she had sacrificed. My dad would say to me, "you don't have to go" when I would express not wanting to leave home for school each time I left. He would tell me you can come home each time I called him from Boston, sick, and rundown. I made it through those next four years and landed a job in Los Angeles after my senior year of college. I did it. Then the 1994

Northridge Earthquake happened. When my mother saw the news and my street on fire, she said to my aunt, "Chris is coming home."

She never asked me. She would never do that. But with my workplace and apartment both in rubble, the sign came that it was ok to go. Again, another gift from God to allow me that time to never regret coming home and to be the lecturer I am today. My purpose is to inspire my son and others to let go of their grief and fear to embrace the gifts given as they appear on their own path to enlightenment.

DAVID GRANT

November 11, 2010
Main Street, Salem, NH
49 years old

I was cycling on the main street of our town. A newly-licensed teenage driver T-boned me. I sustained a traumatic brain injury. I learned that the human spirit is incredibly resilient. That the capacity to overcome the odds dwells within each of us. That what others may perceive to be incredibly hardship can actually be an asset to help others!

Today I live a life I had never planned on living. My experience with traumatic brain injury, from an insider's perspective, has made me acutely aware of the millions who suffer in silence. Since my accident, I have become a tireless advocate for those affected by TBI/Concussion. Over the years since my accident, I have authored two books about life after brain injury. My written work has since been featured in the Chicken Soup for the Soul series. My wife and I now travel the country as I present in a keynote capacity at statewide conferences to help others understand this "invisible disability."

Recovery is a family affair as my wife Sarah and I now publish a monthly magazine, read worldwide, that offers hope and inspiration to those who need it most. Sarah founded a local support group for family members of those who live daily with the challenges that a brain injury brings, and we are both building our new lives by serving others.

The Power of Forgiveness
He almost killed me back in 2010. But if I saw him today, I would most likely give him a hug.

And thank him.

Having a near-death experience does tend to change your outlook on the world. An endurance cyclist for many years, I was out cycling on a typical late fall day in central New England. It was one of those days that most likely drove Robert Frost to write. In fact, I was only a few miles from his birthplace when my life took a bit of an unexpected turn.

Strike that. It was more of an unexpected crash.

No one gets up in the morning wondering if the day will wind down with an ambulance ride and a trip to the nearest trauma center.

But on November 11, 2010, that was to be my fate.

Local authorities estimate that the teenage driver who broadsided me was moving along somewhere between 30 – 40 MPH when we met. He was in a small car – I was on my trusty bike.

When car hits cyclist in a battle of metal vs. metal, the cyclist rarely wins.
Rushed by ambulance across state lines to the trauma center, my wife Sarah following the ambulance, not knowing the condition of her husband, our two vehicle convoy came roaring into the ER. The impact was violent, it was horrific and it was painful. The windshield of the car that hit me was pushed right into the passenger's seat. A first responder later shared that anyone in that seat would have been gravely injured.

Thank God for not-so-small miracles.

My injuries were extensive. Broken bones, torn tendons, and head-to-toe bruises. For the next several days, my wife pulled shards of glass from my head.
And the icing on this accident cake? A traumatic brain injury.

A medical professional, a full year after that November day, let me know in no uncertain terms that my life would never be the same. In fact, he labeled me "permanently disabled."

It's been five years since that fated day – five of the most difficult years, the most glorious years, and the most unexpected years of my life. As predicted, my bruises faded from black to yellow to gone. My bones mended, and the visible signs of my accident faded from the public eye.

But living with a traumatic brain injury, well… to say that life has become a challenge would be an understatement of truly epic proportion. A hale and hearty case of PTSD only added to the mix.

Many things that I used to take for granted, things like knowing the day of the week, what season we are in, or even how to read, have become challenges.

I hold no bitterness toward the young man who careened into me. To hold any bitterness, animosity or resentment bars me from moving forward in my own life. Everyone has "stuff." If you have a heartbeat, life has thrown you a curve ball or two. It's part of our shared human experience.

I've seen close friends lose parents.
And children.
Many I know battle life-threatening or life-changing chronic illnesses.
And some of us get hit by cars at the prime of our lives.
The biggest question is this: Will I let my life experience, no matter how painful, pull me down or lift me up?

I've seen many who chose to be beaten by life's hardships. They wander around, melancholy at what they've lost, willing to tell their own tale of woe to anyone who will listen.

Thanks but no thanks.

Life is indeed for the living. It has taken me many years to come to grips with the fact that life as I knew it is gone. This was not an overnight process. There were peaks and valleys, wonderful days and months defined by ever-present thoughts of suicide.

But out of every season of living when fate seems harsh, new lessons were learned and new strength to be found.

Life today is vastly different than I ever envisioned. Most of my time these days is spent in advocating for those impacted by traumatic brain injury. From one-one-one working with others who share my fate to multiple keynote presentations at medical conferences, the life that I live today simply astounds me.

I have emerged as a new person with a new mission. My experience as a brain injury survivor has made me uniquely qualify to serve others. My written work about life as a true survivor has been read around the world.

On occasion, I think about the young man who forever changed my life. Initially he impacted just one life. But the events that unfolded that day have now touched the lives of tens of thousands.

Occasionally, I think of how my life might have unfolded had I chose to hold on to anger, to not forgive the young man who has unknowingly affected the lives of so many. Had I chosen that path, misery and discontentment would now define my life. This I know as surely as I breathe as I have seen others who have not been able to let to, to forgive, to move on. They live in constant misery.

And the young man who started me on this new, wondrous path of discovery, what ever happened to him?

Humbly I must admit that I tracked him down on Facebook a while ago. If his page is any reflection of his life, he is a student at a local college and moving forward in his life. I remained transparent in my quest to search him out. It is my hope that he rarely thinks about that fall day so many years ago.

And the one time that I did meet him face-to-face in the weeks following my accident, what did I do?

If you guessed that I gave him a hug, you are correct.

David A. Grant

Web: www.metamorphosisbook.com
My TBI Blog: www.DavidsNewLife.com
Facebook: www.facebook.com/TBIHopeandInspiration
Brainline.org: View my Brainline Blog

DENA STEELE

July 1, 2013, on Salem Road in Ralls County, MO. Just a few months before my 43rd birthday, my 15 year old son, Michael, and his 17 year old best friend, Matt, left around 3:30pm in the afternoon to go haul a few bales of hay back from a field about seven miles from our home. Michael was driving the tractor and Matt was sitting at the end of the trailer facing away from Michael. Matt said that he heard Michael yell "help". When he turned and looked, Michael was hanging from the back of the tractor seat. Matt jumped up and ran up to trailer, but before he could get to Michael, he had lost his hold on the seat and fell under the wagon. By the time Matt got the tractor to stop, it was too late. At 4:24pm, my amazing son had passed away. By the time the paramedics came, there was nothing that they could do. He was officially pronounced dead at 5:33pm due to sever head trauma.

Some random things about Michael that I wanted to share: his favorite past time was cutting and splitting wood to sell, he was an expert sharpshooter with both guns and archery, and his favorite things were Dodge Cummins diesel and rebel flags. His favorite show was Duck Dynasty and his favorite clothes were jeans, work boots, and t-shirts with the sleeves cut off. His full name was Michael Alexander Steele and his true love was Kenady Alexandra Johnson. His best friends were: Matthew McGlasson, Brett Hubert, Logan Wayne Boyd, Bobby Burns, Joe Burns, Austin Raddatz, Zeb Finley, and Nicole Steele. Michael always loved to tell jokes and could make anyone laugh. He LOVED to talk to anyone whether he knew them or not and would talk forever! He did not like school and his best features were his smile, and his beautiful brown eyes. Michael's goal was ROTC and to attend WyoTech to learn diesel mechanics. He planned on having a family and naming his children: Austin Michael and Kasey Lea. The thing I miss most about Michael........EVERYTHING.....

Losing Michael has changed my life in so many ways. First & foremost I've learned to live in the moment. No more staring at my phone or watching TV and not focusing on my kids. I no longer take for granted that there will be a tomorrow, another day to spend with my kids, just taking in their presence.
I've learned there may never be a next time to tell your kids that you love them, another chance to hug them, or to hear them say I Love You or just hear their voice at all. There will never be another chance for memories to be made, no more pictures to be taken, no more milestones in life that my son should be here

to achieve.

I've learned not to get upset over trivial things that mean nothing when it's all said and done. I cherish every previous moment with my daughter now.
I never let her go now without saying I Love You and giving her a hug goodbye, because it's always in the back of my mind that this may be the last time I see her, or hear her voice.

I went from being a laid-back, go-with- the-flow mom to now suffering from severe anxiety, depression, & PTSD. Most days just getting out of bed is a struggle, but I'm slowly getting better.

I am much more spiritual than I was before. I've had so many signs from Michael that give me hope. Hope that someday I'll see him again & never have to let him go.

My new found purpose in life, besides being the best possible mom I can be to my daughter, is to keep Michael's memory alive any way I can.
It's my job to let the world know that my child did exist. I simply can't let him be forgotten. I should be teaching my child about the world, not teaching the world about my child.

Keep On Rollin' Coal Bubba. Love You & Miss You Every Second Of Every Day.

DIANE COHEN

Avé's Hope

Introduction:

I always tell my grandchildren that the only rule in Memere's house is that you don't hurt yourself or anyone else. When one of my grandchildren asks if they can do something that I think might be dangerous, I tell them, "Oh, no, Sweetheart, Memere can't let you do that because if you get hurt real bad, Memere will have to jump off a cliff, because Memere will never be able to live without you."

I know God loves me, and I know he loves me even more than I think he does. So, why did the day come when he took one of my precious grandchildren, forcing me to live without her?

Family Background:

Ours is a blended family. My husband, Bob, and I met in 1984 while each of us was going through a very painful divorce. We were just friends at first – we spent a lot of time crying on each other's shoulders about how we had failed in our marriages. And we cried about how that horrible monster called "divorce" was devouring our children. I had two daughters from my first marriage. Kerri was 10 that year and Amy was 8. Bob's son Nathan was 5 and his daughter Sabrina was 3.

Before long, our friendship grew into a more loving and intimate one. Our ex-spouses remarried shortly after the divorces were final and expanded their families with more children. Bob and I were far more cautious. We didn't want our children to have to "adjust" to yet another change. But raising two sets of children in two separate households was a tremendous financial burden on us. So, after some time had passed, Bob sold his house and moved in with me and my two little girls. Bob's ex-wife had primary custody of his children, but we converted our finished basement into a bedroom for them, and they stayed with us 3 or 4 days per week.

Blending our children was tough, in part because of the differences in their ages, plus the fact that Bob's children were with us only part-time. But Bob and I tried really hard to keep everyone together and to find a common bond among us. That was no easy task, since we ourselves came from very different backgrounds.

Bob was raised in an orthodox Jewish household, and was active in the Synagogue throughout his childhood. He attended Hebrew school and celebrated his bar-mitzvah as a young lad. Bob's parents were very proud of him and frequently delegated to Bob the recitation of traditional Hebrew prayers at family gatherings.

My parents were Catholic and sent me to parochial schools. I attended Mass with my family every Sunday and celebrated all of the sacraments like any good Catholic girl should.

This was all taking place during the tumultuous 60s when young men across America were burning their draft cards and young women were burning their bras. Society was changing real fast, and by the time Bob and I came of age (on separate sides of a fairly large city), religion and all of its rituals fell by the wayside. Thus, when Bob and I met in 1984, we were part of the vast majority of non-worshippers in New England, although we still considered ourselves "Jewish" and "Catholic" respectively; labels our parents had bestowed upon us at birth.

In 1989, my paternal grandmother died. I loved this grandmother but I wouldn't say we were especially close. Nevertheless, her death caused me to start questioning the meaning of life. I felt compelled to return to the Catholic church. I began attending Sunday Mass on a somewhat regular basis, but the void I felt inside seemed to grow larger every day. As I looked around the church, it seemed like everyone was married and I had a big banner on my back that read "divorced." My relationship with Bob started to fall apart as I became aware of the sin in my life. I had divorced the father of my children and was living with a man who was not my husband. We were sleeping in the same bed, in plain view of our young impressionable children. The guilt was eating away at me.

Bob and I talked at great length about this. We knew we couldn't reverse the past, but perhaps we could make the future better. So, in 1990, we decided to legitimize our blended family by getting married. We flew to Florida with our four kids, dressed them up in wedding finery, and got married on a small island off the Gulf of Mexico by a justice of the peace, surrounded by a handful of our closest family and friends. My daughters, Kerri and Amy, now aged 16 and 14 served as my bridesmaids, Nathan served as his father's "best man" at the ripe old age of 10, and little Sabrina, age 8, was our flower girl. Our wedding cake was decorated with the traditional bride and groom on the top, but we also added small figurines of our children standing alongside us. We wanted the kids to know that we were getting married as a family. After the wedding, we took the kids with us on a honeymoon vacation to Walt Disney World.

When we returned to our home state of New Hampshire, we continued on with our daily routine of working and raising kids. Bob and I were getting along great, but I still felt a terrible void in my heart, like God was calling me to something else. The long dark cold New England winters were taking a toll on me and I began suffering from Seasonal Affective Disorder (SAD) a form of depression caused by lack of sufficient sunlight. My parents had retired to Florida and I missed them more than I ever thought possible. Bob and I were working in Nashua, New Hampshire for a Florida real estate developer at the time. We coordinated flights for people desiring to purchase real estate in the sunshine state. Occasionally, we were allowed to accommodate our clients on the weekend fly-and-buy trips, which I loved because it took me away from the freezing cold, and allowed me to visit with my parents who had purchased a new home in the very community we were marketing.

But 1990 was a bad year for the New Hampshire economy, and by the Spring of 1991, the development company Bob and I worked for closed its Nashua office and relocated its marketing department to Florida. We had only been married for one year, and still struggling financially when we suddenly found ourselves both jobless in an economy that was rapidly collapsing. We tried finding new jobs, but it just wasn't happening. Our home went into foreclosure and we were forced to declare bankruptcy.

I spoke to my parents about our dilemma and they suggested that we move to Florida. The thought appealed to me a great deal, but Bob wasn't so sure about it. He was afraid he would miss his children too much, since they would be staying in New Hampshire with their mother who had primary custody. Still, we knew we had little choice. So, we came up with a compromise. I would go to Florida, stay with my parents, and begin searching for a job. Bob would stay in New Hampshire with the four kids, and look for a job too. We agreed that the first one of us to find a new job that would support the family would be the determining factor as to whether we would relocate to Florida or stay in New Hampshire. Not long after I arrived in Florida, I was hired by the same developer for whom Bob and I had worked in New Hampshire. I rented a newly-built house about a mile from my parents' home, and Bob and I began the task of moving our family to Florida, both physically and emotionally. To say that process was tough is a tremendous understatement. My daughter, Kerri, a senior in high school, begged me to let her stay in New Hampshire so she could graduate with her friends. Nathan and Sabrina begged their Daddy not to move so far away. We were so torn between the need to support our family and the guilt we felt at forcing the kids to endure another adjustment in their lives. In the end we agreed to let Kerri move into her father's house so she could stay in New Hampshire for her last year of high school; and we set aside a certain amount of money in our budget so Bob could fly to New Hampshire once every six weeks to see Nathan and Sabrina, and to fly them to Florida during school breaks. Amy was entering her freshman year of high school, and was a more adventurous type than her older sister, so the timing was good for her. She was excited about starting school in a new state and meeting new friends.

Shortly after we began our new lives in Florida, I was invited to a woman's Christmas social by a co-worker. The event was taking place at a Presbyterian church in Lecanto, Florida. I wasn't sure what to expect, but I was eager to fill the void that still haunted me, so I agreed to go. To my delight, I enjoyed a most amazing evening of music, testimony, and prayer. The void I felt in my heart began to fill with a joy I had never before experienced. I was overwhelmed with the sense that something awesome was happening in this church and I needed to be part of it.

The following Sunday, Bob and I began attending the weekly services. He was somewhat reluctant at first, thinking it was just another one of my whims that I would soon get over. But for the first two Sundays after leaving the service, we cried in the car all the way home as we discussed the message we had heard and how it applied in our lives. We both felt that we were hearing the truth about God in a way we had never heard before. Shortly thereafter, we signed up for the 8-week Pastor's Class to see if we could become members of this church. I was gung-ho, but Bob was more reticent. He was having trouble reconciling the idea of being "born again" with the "chosen" nature of his Jewish heritage. The first night of Pastor's Class, Bob said to me, "You know, Di, I've been a Jew for 41 years, don't expect me to become a Christian in 8 weeks." I assured Bob that I had no expectations for him. I knew that God was in charge and that his will would prevail for both of us. Eight weeks later, we were both accepted into membership at Seven Rivers Presbyterian Church and were baptized as new creatures in Christ.

From that day forward, everything began to change. Just before Thanksgiving in 2002, an amazing thing happened in our family. All four of our children were now grown and living in the northeast – even Amy who moved to upstate New York after college. Each of our kids had become involved with a "significant other" and we wanted all eight of them to join us in Florida for Thanksgiving that year. Bob and I talked about the sleeping arrangements. None of the kids were married, and we weren't trying to be "holier-than-thou" but we also didn't want to be presumptuous about whether or not they were sleeping with their significant others, plus we wanted to set a good example for them. Fortunately, we had a four-bedroom house, so Bob and I went to a furniture rental store, and rented two sets of bunk beds. They were delivered to the house and we set them up in one of the bedrooms. This was going to be the "boys" room. Our son, Nathan, would share this room with John, Pete, and Ross, the boyfriends of our three daughters. Meanwhile, two of our daughters would sleep in another bedroom, and the other daughter would sleep with Krysten, our son's girlfriend, in a separate bedroom. When all the kids arrived that Thanksgiving, they were quite taken aback by the sleeping arrangements. But they respected our wishes and assumed their assigned bunks. At the Thanksgiving table the next day, Bob thanked God for bringing all four of our kids to us for this special meal, and also thanked him for bringing John, Pete, Ross, and Krysten into our lives. We had no idea where these new relationships were headed, but we knew that God was using us in some way to accomplish his will. The whole weekend was filled with fun and laughter as we got to know the four new kids that had joined our family for this special time. By the end of the weekend, all eight of the kids had affectionately nicknamed the weekend "Camp Thanksgiving." And within the next five years, every one of our children had married the "significant other" they had brought to Camp Thanksgiving.

Eventually, Bob and I built a house near the beach in New Hampshire so we could have a family home nearer to our grown children. We split our time between New Hampshire and Florida for many years, and eventually sold our house in Florida and returned to New Hampshire full time. The kids come home for holidays and summer vacations, and when the suggestion was made to name our beach house as so many coastal dwellers do, the kids unanimously christened it "Camp Thanksgiving."

Avé Hope Dugas:
Within a span of ten years, God had blessed Bob and I with the birth of nine grandchildren. Our youngest grandchild, Avé Hope Dugas, was born on May 15, 2013. She was a beautiful, full-term, healthy baby girl, the second child born

to our daughter, Sabrina, and her husband, Ross. The first few months of Avé's life flew quickly and her smiles and coos were the delight of the whole family.

One gray October day, Sabrina was suffering from mastitis and decided to stay home from work. She brought Avé and her 3-year-old sister, Lilah, to daycare as usual, hoping that she would get some much needed rest. Around 5 o'clock in the afternoon, we received a frantic call from Sabrina, hysterically screaming that she had just received a call from the day care center informing her that Avé was non-responsive. 911 had been called and Sabrina was on her way to the hospital, praying and screaming for God to save her precious baby girl. We immediately jumped into our van and drove the 45 minutes to Manchester. As we prayed along the way, we sent text messages to our three older kids urging them to pray too. When we arrived at the hospital, our son-in-law Ross greeted us in the emergency room and sadly announced that Baby Avé didn't make it. She was now in heaven with Jesus. "No, no, no. No, this can't be, I said." My husband held me tightly. "She's in heaven now, Bob sobbed." "No. No. Not one of our grandchildren. No," I continued. I entered the triage room to find our inconsolable daughter laying in a hospital bed with her precious 4-month old resting motionless beside her. I bent over the bed to kiss Sabrina and assure her that this could not be real. No mother should ever have to go through this. Sabrina was such an attentive mother – almost to a fault. She was neither a drinker, nor a smoker, and during her pregnancies she took the extra step of avoiding any food items that might even remotely be linked to birth defects. "Not Sabrina, not Avé, no God, no," I demanded!

The pastor from Sabrina and Ross' church arrived with a couple of associate pastors. We gathered with them around the hospital bed, and sent our grieving prayer requests to our heavenly father. I knew that our precious little Avé was resting in the arms of Jesus, but my heart still ached for her, and I didn't want her death to be real. But it was real. We would later learn that Avé died from Sudden Unexplained Infant Death Syndrome (SUIDS).

Avé's funeral was held a week later. The strength of our family was evident as we drew closer than we had ever been before. We reflected on the events that brought us to this day. We sobbed together, we prayed together, and we dreamed about the day when Jesus would return to earth and make sense of this horrible tragedy. I wondered how I would explain Avé's death to our other grandchildren.

Three-year-old Lilah, bright and precocious, at times seemed to understand that her baby sister had gone to heaven to live with Jesus. But moments later, she would ask Mommy and Daddy when Avé was coming home. The rest of our grandchildren, likewise, were saddened. Our 7-year-old grandson, Michael, was particularly affected. The day he heard the news, he sat under a blanket in his room for hours, crying for Avé. On the day of the funeral, Michael presented Auntie Sabrina with a picture book he had made the day Mommy told him that Baby Avé had gone to heaven. On the front cover, using only black crayon, Michael had drawn a large group of people. The smallest person in the group was a baby at the bottom center of the picture. Using a red crayon, Michael had drawn a big red smile on the baby's face. "This is our family" Michael explained, "and this is Baby Avé." Michael is a very smart and sensitive boy and somehow he knew that while we were all grieving as a family, Baby Avé was perfectly happy. That drawing will remain imprinted on my heart and in my mind forever.

The night of the funeral, our two daughters, Kerri and Amy, together with their husbands and children spent the night at Camp Thanksgiving with Bob and I. At the time, both girls had a 5-year-old son: Andrew lived in New York and Joshua lived in New Hampshire. But despite the miles between them, these two little rascals were the best of buddies. At family gatherings, they played together constantly, picking up where they left off as if no time had passed. The night of the funeral, as I was tucking Joshua into bed, he asked me, "Memere, where is Baby Avé?" I replied, "Well, Josh, Baby Avé is in heaven with Jesus now. Someday we're going to go to heaven too; and someday, Jesus is going to bring all of us back to earth, and there's going to be a new earth, and everything is going to be wonderful and nobody is ever going to die again." Those words seemed to quiet Joshua, so I kissed him goodnight, and left the room. The next morning, Joshua and Andrew were the first ones up to greet me in the kitchen. As they sat at the breakfast counter chatting, I scrambled up a couple of eggs for them. I had no idea how seriously Joshua had taken my words of the night before, until he suddenly announced to his cousin, "Andrew, when we come back to the new earth, I want you to live next to me."

I closed my eyes and thanked God for the faith of a small child. Joshua never questioned my response of the night before, he simply accepted it in faith. And faith was the very thing that kept me from jumping off a cliff in my time of grief.

Three months later, our family gathered at Camp Thanksgiving for our annual Christmas celebration. We have a tradition in our family that dates back to when

Bob and I met in 1984. The two of us had taken a trip out to California to visit Bob's uncle. While there, we stopped in a Christmas shop in San Francisco, and purchased four moose ornaments for our children personalized with their names. Every Christmas thereafter, the children enjoyed hanging their moose ornaments on the tree. In 2003 when our daughter, Amy, married John, it seemed appropriate that John should also have a personalized moose to hang on the tree, so we purchased one for him. John would later tease the boyfriends of Kerri and Sabrina, and the girlfriend of Nathan, that someday if they were lucky enough to join this family in marriage, they might get their own personalized moose to hang on the tree. Sure enough, it happened in 2005 that Kerri married Pete and that Christmas Pete received his personalized moose to hang on the tree. In 2006, Krysten earned her moose, followed by Ross in 2007. Each moose was carefully selected to reflect the individual personalities of our adult "children" and, the annual tradition of the hanging of the moose continues each year, with the newest member of the family hanging his or her moose first. In 2004, our first grandchild, Johnny, was assisted by his parents in hanging his personalized moose; followed by Ella and Michael in 2006, Andrew and Joshua in 2008; Camden in 2009, Lilah in 2010, and Molly in 2011.

Avé was born in May 2013. In September of that year, Bob and I took a vacation to Alaska. Browsing through the gift shops it occurred to us that we needed to find a moose ornament for Avé. Alaska has a great selection of moose ornaments but we wanted to find just the right one to fit Avé's personality. Bob picked out a pretty little moose ornament with angel wings. We both loved it but discounted it as inappropriate. Still, as we continued browsing through the wide variety of ornaments, we were constantly drawn back to the angel moose. So much so, that we decided, "let's get it." Little did we know that one month later, our precious Avé would indeed become our little angel, so it was most fitting at Christmas that year to present Sabrina and Ross with Avé's personalized moose ornament to be hung on the tree. They were so grateful that we included Avé in this most cherished of family traditions, and the story of how we came to choose the little moose with the angel wings proved to be nothing short of divine intervention.

Just before Christmas that same year, my daughter-in-law Krysten called to ask if I was going to have a Christmas stocking hung for Avé. Every year since our first grandchild was born, a stocking is hung from the fireplace mantel with a Christmas character of some sort embellished on the front. There are Santas and snowmen and reindeer appliquéd on a background of red, blue or green felt, and each child's name is stitched at the top. I told Krysten that I wasn't sure if a stocking for Avé was a good idea because I didn't want Sabrina to feel sad at the sight of Avé's empty stocking while all the other children's stockings were filled with toys and goodies. Krysten suggested that we all participate in "stuffing" Avé's stocking with donations for research on SIDS (Sudden Infant Death Syndrome) and SUIDS (Sudden Unexplained Infant Death Syndrome.) She added that even the grandchildren could participate by decorating envelopes containing money from their piggy banks. I loved the idea, so Krysten took charge of notifying the other family members of the plan, and I picked up a white felt Christmas stocking for Ave, embellished it with an angel on the front, and stitched her name across the top to match those of the other grandkids. At our family Christmas party that year, when Bob announced that it was time to hand out the stockings, everyone watched as Sabrina and Ross were presented with Avé's angel stocking. Tears welled up in all of our eyes as Sabrina and Ross began removing the donations made in Avé's honor. The grandkids had written Avé's name on their envelopes and decorated them with colorful drawings to which they added glitter and little pompoms. They were so excited about this moment, they hardly remembered that they had stockings coming to them as well.

Later in the day, I sat at the dining room table with Sabrina, Krysten, Kerri and Amy. We talked about the emotions of being a mother and how losing a baby was possibly the most painful thing any mother could ever endure, but none of us knew that better than Sabrina. In truth, we couldn't even imagine how she felt. Sabrina thanked us for not forgetting about Avé. She was so grateful that we had included Avé in all the Christmas traditions at Camp Thanksgiving. We assured Sabrina that keeping Avé's memory alive was something we were all committed to. Avé was a very important person in our family, and she would remain so forever.

Some months later, Bob and I, together with Sabrina, Ross, and Ross' Dad, Gary, established Avé's Hope, Inc., a non-profit organization to raise money for SIDS and SUIDS research. Each Christmas, family members "stuff" Avé's stocking with donations, and all funds go directly to Dr. Hannah Kinney at Boston Children's Hospital who has dedicated her career to researching the causes of SIDS and SUIDs.

Conclusion:
Over the years our faith has taught Bob and I that God's purpose for us on this earth is to form relationships. Through our relationships, we learn to carry one

another's burdens and grow stronger in faith along the way. Ultimately, God will call us into perfect relationship with him in heaven and eternally on the new earth. We look forward to being reunited with Baby Avé at that time. In the meantime, we encourage you to visit our website at www.aveshope.org, and send us your personal stories about SIDS or SUIDS for possible publication on our site. Anyone wishing to make donations to Avé's Hope, Inc. may do so on the website.

About the author:

Diane Cohen is a Florida lawyer practicing in the area of wills, trusts, and probate. She lives in Hampton, New Hampshire with her husband Bob and travels to Florida on a regular basis to meet with clients. She believes that God has blessed her with life experiences that uniquely enable her to compassionately work with families during times of grief and sorrow.

DONNA BROTHERS

May 30, 1987
Birmingham, Alabama
I was 21 years old.

My mother, brother, and sister were all jockeys before me, so I grew up watching horse races and somewhat surrounded by jockeys. Having so many jockeys around me took the fascination out of it for me, and led me to falsely believe that riding a race must not be very difficult. When I rode my first race, I was immediately blown away by the rapidity of the action. Within the first second of breaking from the starting gate, the horses and jockeys are literally jockeying for position and once you're behind some of the other horses, dirt is flying back with both speed and velocity. Nothing can really prepare you for how much dirt flies back and it took a real mental effort to stop flinching and blinking rapidly. I had to tell myself, "its ok! I have goggles on!" Once I adjusted to that, I realized my horse was looking for some direction from me, so I had to access the situation around me and the horse, underneath me, and start actually riding the race rather than being a passenger. By the time the race was finished I had a new respect for my brother, sister, and mother. Not only was riding a race the most exciting thing I had ever done, it was also the most challenging. I chose this as my "second" because that one race started me on my path to a successful career as a thoroughbred jockey.

I learned not to judge a book by its cover and to never try to imagine what someone else's job or life is like unless you've actually done it. Before actually riding a race, I had so many misconceptions about what it would be like. And if I had continued to judge that option falsely without ever having tried it, I would've missed out on the greatest ride of my life.

I also learned, as time went on, that there was a direct correlation between how hard I worked and how "lucky" I got.

I further learned that we have only one thing in life within our control: our word. Our word creates our reputation and our credibility—two things that, once soiled, one may spend a lifetime trying to restore. Keep your word and your reputation and credibility will follow.

Oh gosh, I cannot imagine what my life would've been like had I not become a jockey but I can only imagine that it would not have been nearly as rich or as fulfilling.

2710 Birmingham   7/9/87
TRACE OF MAGIC.....Second
MAYME'S TEA.........Third

DISCOVER ACRO
JOCKEYS FIRST WIN
1 Mile   1:42.4

Chuck Deupree.......Owner
Tony Cataldi......Trainer
Donna Barton..........up

DONNA G. PAUL

The Voice

How I longed to hear his voice again. I heard it for the first time almost forty years earlier—deep and compelling. It echoed through my dreams, often waking me inside a frenzied clutch. Repeatedly I pushed it away until the haunting memory of its sound washed over my heart again a few nights later. Every year that passed confirmed I could never find its owner. I didn't even know his name; just that he had beautiful dark hair and very pink cheeks, yet somehow I loved him. And in the dark, I prayed for his safekeeping.

Then, his phone call. June 17, 2004, 5:03 pm. His resonant voice filled the second my life changed forever and led to the magical minute I learned he had longed for the sound of mine. The incredible hour he described the years he searched, all the while trying to envision me. He spoke about how he wondered where I was, what I did, who had I become.

That beautiful crystalline evening our words ran ahead, colliding and splashing through our tears. If one could color conversations, ours would be bright yellow with vivid blue and red jagged streaks where we laughed in delight, then sobbed and confessed our longing for this moment. There must also be an angry slash of dark gray near the center. It would appear as I confessed to dreams of seeing him again, but never daring to take any action that might bring me closer to this kind of reality.

Drained and exhausted from the adrenalin rush, I hated when the call ended. Until he promised another call the next day, as well as an assurance that he had a plane ticket. We would see one another in two weeks.

Beginning the next morning and occurring several times a day thereafter, every phone call revealed more intrigue. We both loved swimming, mountains, and dogs. Lasagna, peanut butter cookies, honey mustard dressing. We'd both wondered at hundreds of moons; was it shining on him or her as we watched? Our tears of joy and relief continued, and our glee bubbled up soft or wild and raucous.

Between phone calls we exchanged emails and photos. My goodness, he was handsome. I smiled at the same dark hair and pink cheeks I'd seen across the room long ago. In fact, I smiled at everything these days. I could no more stop grinning than breathing.

He lived in a state I'd never visited; said he never imagined me in Texas. We had loving families. We came from good places in life.

We called each other at all hours. Every time I spoke with him, I came away breathless and filled with longing for his touch, his scent, his presence. Words still flew out of me before my brain could catch them as the days passed. The big day arrived. I expected him by eight that night.

* * *

He was more than an hour late. Beside me, the phone sat rigid and silent. Several times I thought I heard an approaching car, but no lights appeared in the driveway. To be certain, I hurried to the door and looked up the lane. Outlines of pine trees stretched straight against the dark, cradling the lonely, empty road. Back inside, I paced, licked my dry lips and fretted.

I imagined his flight was delayed, a foul up with the car rental, or he stopped to eat along the way. Dallas traffic can be brutal; that could be the problem. Perhaps he had taken a wrong turn. Still, sending directions to strangers is part of my job, and mine are explicit.

I had not talked with him since the evening before. Maybe he hadn't packed his cell phone. Another hour passed. It was easy for me to picture his journey going very wrong. I envisioned him changing a flat tire as eighteen-wheelers spewed stinking heat from the pavement while whizzing close. In another vivid scenario, I saw a skidding car, flashing lights and an unresponsive victim unable to use that deep soft voice to tell a kind stranger, "I'm on my way to meet…"

Worst of all, could he be sitting in a bar somewhere, nursing a beer and wondering if he really did want to see me after all this time?

I would not allow doubt to seep over me. I would not believe he had changed his mind and was not coming that night. Or never. I forced myself to be positive; he would be here in less than five minutes. Just enough time to put on a little lipstick and blush.

To be sure, though, I squeezed my eyes shut and prayed. "Please God, keep him safe, but let him get here soon."

The instant I added thanks to the Lord for all my blessings and opened my eyes, lights swept across the living room wall. Through the window I saw a car turn down my drive. I hurried outside. The car shuddered as the transmission clunked and the driver's door popped open. I made it to the back of the car as its brake lights flashed.

He hurled himself toward me.

I had no time to marvel, no time to regret weighing more than ever, or not having my roots darkened. No time to look into that beautiful face and cup it between my hands. Wrapped in the strongest embrace I'd ever felt, I was smothered in a dozen kisses. I stood still, rooted to the pavement and floating above the stars.

Tears sprang to my eyes. My mind emptied as I relished the feel of him holding me close. I knew I should take a step back and invite him inside, but I couldn't let go. I felt him shaking—or was that me?

My mind raced my heart. I could only choke out a few words; "I thought you'd never get here. Oh, honey, I can't believe it—you're finally here."
Impressive statements.

My lack of makeup, appropriate sentiment, or even decorum did not seem to matter. I heard his now familiar voice murmuring into the hollow between my neck and shoulder. "I've looked for you my whole life and I finally found you."

My heart beat hard, my breaths came in ragged shudders. God had finally answered my prayers. The voice I heard all those years ago belonged to the man before me.

This moment would forever blot out the haunting agony of hearing his cries fade down the hall as a nurse carried him from the delivery room to another life.

No phrase could be more exquisite than his next: "I love you, Mom."

* * *

I waited patiently for the LORD; he inclined to me and heard my cry. He drew me up from the pit of destruction, out of the miry bog, and set my feet upon a rock, making my steps secure. He put a new song in my mouth, a song of praise to our God. Many will see and fear, and put their trust in the LORD. Psalm 40:1-3

Vindication arrived after thirty-eight years of longing for forgiveness. Through God's grace and mercy, my life changed forever. A dozen years later, Joel and I still wonder at the bonds and traits we share. His finding me expanded the love holding our entire family together. He, Jonathan, and Stephanie bonded like triplets and talk often.

When I look into the night sky and see the moon, I say a mother's prayer of thanks because I know it's shining on Joel too.

And, yes, I still smile when I hear his typical rich greeting, "Hi Mom. Just called to say I love you."

EILEEN DOYON

Mary Ann "Marie" Guillily Donbeck

It was September, 1963, Labor Day Weekend. We had rented the usual log home on Lake George, New York. Along with the home, we had a speedboat , and friends and family would come and visit and share in the fun on the lake.

For whatever reason that year, we decided to stay through Labor Day Weekend when most people had packed up and went back to their own home to get ready for school to start. My dad left to check on some job sites he was working on. He owned a roofing, sheet metal business. My two older brothers decided to take a ride together on their motorcycle. I was playing out by the lake and decided to go in and get something to eat for lunch. It was chilly that morning and there was a fire burning in the fireplace that my dad lite before he left. When I came through the front door, my mom wanted to get a better fire going to ease off the chill for us at lunchtime. I was standing right next to my mom and she took a can of lighter fluid in her hand and squeezed the can on to the fire. Out shot the lighter fluid. That was my second my life changed forever. A spark flew back at my mom hitting the lighter fluid can and it exploded in her hand. She went up literally up in flames. She ran out the back door screaming. All I saw were flames all over my mom. I ran out the front door with only a burn on my hand. Then, I ran out to the backyard and there was my mom rolling in dirt to put the fire out that was covering her body. I was kneeling by her side picking up dirt and throwing it on her too. She said to go get help. My mission began. I went from house to house screaming, yelling, and pounding on doors and windows but everyone was gone. I ran up the street further and further as fast as I could and then heard my brothers' motorcycle coming down the road. I started screaming and crying trying to tell them what just happened to our mom. I can still see the looks on both my brother's faces clear as day. They took off on their motorcycle and headed back to the camp. They were 11 and 13. By the time I got back to the camp, my mom was sitting under a birch tree with people all around her and then the ambulance took her away. The fire department was there putting the fire out. The next thing I remember was...... my dad...... he pulled up, got out of his truck and then I saw his face. I ran to him and he picked me up but only for a second. He tried to get all the facts as to what just happened. I do not remember much the next few days.

The following week, my dad asked me if I wanted to go to see my mom, she was asking for me. "YES" came immediately out of my mouth. It was just me and my dad and he did not say much to me on the drive to the hospital. He had to sneak me into ICU after 8pm. Kids were not allowed in the hospital back then and never in ICU. Visiting hours ended at 8pm. He snuck me thru the kitchen at Glens Falls Hospital and the people were so nice to me and then we had to take the "special" elevator. It was the "service" one. I did not know the difference, I just felt that I was special.

I remember walking into ICU. Beds were lined up all along the walls. There were no private rooms for ICU back then. My dad brought me over to a bed and it was my mom......I did not recognize her. Her body was burnt all over except her face. Her hair was all gone. She suffered 2nd and 3rd degree burns. I could tell my mom was in so much pain.

It was decided that I would stay with my Uncle Bill and Aunt Anna along with my cousin for the time being. I wish that decision was never made. Looking back now, I just wanted, and needed to be around my dad and my brothers..... my family, but I had no choice. I loved my aunt and uncle dearly and I am sure it was challenging for my cousin who was a few years older than me. My Uncle Bill became my second dad. He was always so funny. We had so much fun, and my Aunt Anna made the best apple pies! I lived with them for about a year and a half. I became a loner then and had to learn to take care of myself at six years old. I always felt like an outsider from that point on. For Thanksgiving, the hospital let my mom come home for a holiday celebration. My dad had everything catered by Chateau D' Louis in South Glens Falls. The ambulance brought my mom to our house and she could only stay for a short time. She looked like a mummy all wrapped in bandages. How it must have been so painful. My mom had to learn to walk all over again. She had a lot of skin grafting done and never, never did I hear my mom complain or cry. I got to know all the service people and nurses in the hospital. They knew how bad my mom was burnt and how long she was in the hospital and I was the late night guest. I kept myself entertained and never really understood all that was happening. I would go with my dad to visit but had the run of the hospital. I remember the café to the right when you walked into the hospital with the big white glass doors.....most of the staff knew me and were so nice. I wished I could have stopped that second from ever happening. It was devastating to my mom and our family life changed forever. When I moved back into my own home from my aunt and uncle's, everything was different. Being separated from my family was so hard and especially during a tragedy. I just wanted to be at my own home with my mom and dad and brothers. Since that did not happen for me, I learned how to adjust and became self-sufficient in many areas of my life at six years old. That molded me to be independent, block out things and people, and be on my own to keep the pain out.

Now being in my 50's, I better understand myself. It's the family lessons that we learn from and we create our core, if you will, or at least I did. My mom and I were never close afterwards. I hate myself for that, but she was dealing with her own life and suffering, and I was somewhat protecting myself being self-sufficient. Sometimes it came across as being selfish, but unfortunately in life, we learn to survive during situations that happen to us. The survival mode. That second changed my life forever and the lessons that I learned, I learned late in life. Family must always stick together thru the thick and thin when crap happens. The good news is….at least God has given me the knowledge to realize it now in my life……so I can be a better person and help others as best I can. My mom died in July/1981 of a massive heart attack at the age of 58. Miss you mom……and love you dearly………

ERICA ARGY

Feb 7, 2012
Syracuse, New York
I was 31

The day was a very blurry yet emotional one. I was told by the hospice nurse she didn't have much longer. How can you digest those words and prepare yourself to let go of the woman who raised you. I didn't want to believe it. I didn't want to have to go on without her. I had to say goodbye to my mother who was dying from breast cancer. I had to lie and tell her I was going to be ok and in those last words I said I love you Mom, it's ok to let go, I will be ok. She took her last breath at 5:13 pm and died in my arms.

My life was changed forever. I went through extreme depression. I blamed myself for her death I felt guilt and anger. I kicked my boyfriend out and told myself I was ok. Well a few months after it all came down on me. My reality caught up and smacked me in the face. My mother was dead! I'm feeling this way because she wants me with her. I ended up in a local hospital and received the treatment I needed. To this day I'm still suffering from PTSD and depression.
To trust myself and know what I am feeling is true. Don't try to deny it. Don't fake a smile. Know there are people out there that have been in your shoes and can help you through grieving.

I'm a different person today as I was 4 years ago. I will always have a piece of my heart that is not here. I have come to know that death is always something that can never be avoided. I will always struggle with certain memories that will shut me down for days, but then I know I have to be strong for my family and just know she still lives on in my heart.

ERIN MUSTO

In a moment or even just a millisecond, life can change. Life is like that. Little things can change our life and perspective in huge ways; sometimes those moments change us for forever.

I remember the last time I blinked as a whole person, as a mom who had it all. It seems like 100 years ago- time doesn't really work the same for me anymore. On February 2, 2012 we woke up like normal; drank our coffee and made breakfast like normal… but under that normal there was worry and fear for many potential symptoms our daughter Madeline was experiencing. I made arrangements for her sisters so my husband, Madeline and I could head to a doctor's appointment. We hoped this appointment would clear up our worries. In those moments I knew it had to be anemia or a deficiency… something treatable and fixable. Madeline was a child and children get fixed. We visited our Pediatrician, went over our compiled list of potential symptoms in recent days, he assessed Madeline's lack of strength and ability to walk. He told us he really didn't know what the problem was. He offered blood work or to head to the ER for answers. We hopped in the car and hurried to Albany Med to sit in the Emergency Room and wait……..

Sitting with Madeline as she grew more tired and weaker by the moment, waiting to see a doctor, were some of the hardest moments. My brain knew it was serious but my heart and soul couldn't know it yet, it wasn't time. We finally got a room, a CT scan and then an MRI… all big scary steps. Sitting in the huge waiting room waiting for Madeline to come out of her MRI was torture. I remember sitting against the wall, feeling weak and empty watching the door for the doctor to come out. It took so long to get to recovery to see her, it was like time slow down to a snail's pace…

I slept next to Madeline that night, on a bed full of monitors and cords and a tiny weak Madeline. I remember waking up to Madeline right with me, my back killed, my body was squashed into the crack between the bed and wall. I stayed in that spot, right next to Madeline waiting…

What seemed like hours later, but could have been minutes, a room of doctors walked in and we were ushered into the hall to talk and look at the scans. My life changed completely in those moments, those milliseconds of life. I kept waiting to hear 'it's going to be all right' or 'Mrs. Musto she'll be fine'... but instead we were greeted with the scariest words ever spoken to a parent. "Your child has cancer, terminal cancer." A tumor had formed in Madeline's brainstem, a spider web shaped tumor. Madeline's diagnosis was a rare brainstem tumor- a childhood cancer called DIPG, Diffuse Intrinsic Pontine Glioma. DIPG is terminal and mostly untreatable. Our five year old was dying. Our Madeline was fighting a monster which would steal her heartbeat and spirit and life.

I remember standing in the hallway, in shock and full of fear. The doctor said to us "Enjoy this time, there will be lots of time later to be sad and grieve." Those words refocused our attention on Madeline and enjoying the time we had. In only a moment our life was broken, in a few words a little bit of it was patched back together. We enjoyed and celebrated that time with Madeline. Madeline passed only 5 days after diagnosis, only 5 days.

Life changed in a blink... DIPG brought us to the new world of missing and loss and grief. Cancer also brought us a profound reminder to live and enjoy this time here. Madeline isn't here, but she is fine; she is safe, loved and completely okay. She is safe and home, we are just here living, growing and waiting to be home with her. I am broken and saved because of her. I am sad and full of joy- all because in a moment, a tiny millisecond, my whole life changed for worse and for better.

Erin Musto
climbingupthepolkadottree.com

GreenHouse Picker Sisters

We are Holly and Amanda, two women who are on a journey, surrounded by beautiful messes, and still trying to find all the good in the world. And guys, there is still so much good out there just waiting to be uncovered! How do we know this? Because we have experienced it firsthand. Let me explain more by taking you back to two years ago, to January 2014, when our whole entire world changed. When people ask us, "How did you get started?" THIS is the story behind our start. It isn't fluffy and beautiful, but it's our story and we trust God's plan that it will be a beautiful ending to a not so beautiful story.

On January 27th, we got a dreaded phone everyone hopes they'll never receive. The call that our Dad, our hero, at age 49, had had a totally unforeseen massive heart attack, and it did not look good. So our entire family rushed to the hospital where we were told that our father only had 10% function of his heart and would need a heart transplant, and he would not be leaving the hospital until he received one. The shock and the feelings that came with this news were simply unbearable. How could this be happening to him, a very healthy, hard-working, and vibrant man with so much left to give? See, if you knew our Dad, you know he was the bravest, kindest, most caring man you would ever know. He was a man who loved everyone fiercely and with every ounce of his being. He wanted every man or woman to be treated just as well as the next, no matter his or her story or status. He gave endless hours of his life to support local and international ministries, all while working a full time job.

HOW could he be the one suffering and facing his end on this earth? The one who would give his coat off his back to an enemy if they needed it. Oh Jesus, how? Why him? Why now? He is so young? Yet it was our reality, and would be for 3.5 months as we begged God to bring us a miracle. As we waited day after day in the hospital, we experienced an even greater miracle and that was our father. In the midst of surgery after surgery, ups and downs, good news and bad news, it was him who reminded us that we could put all of our trust in his Father, the Prince of Peace. Our father, a tower of strength, was full of true peace, saying many times, "If this is my end, my story, bring me home Jesus. I have no greater love than you. We can't fight this story, if it is my time, He will take me home to be with Him." Many months later and with so much more to tell, this is exactly what Jesus did. He came, wrapped His arms around my father and said, "Well done, good and faithful servant! Now come home." He created him 49 years earlier, and He wanted His son home …he was that special, he was that good, and we had to let him go.

The pain and void of this homecoming was and has been at times, darker than you could ever imagine for all of us. Yet … there still is still so much good to be had. Even in the hospital stay, we witnessed so much good, from nurses, strangers, family, friends, and an entire community, and are still hearing stories of impact that happened during our darkest days!

Four months after his passing, my sister and I both decided that we needed to be part of something bigger than ourselves. We told our husbands our crazy idea and they quickly told us it would never work. So of course, we had to show them they were wrong! We decided to start turning our family's vintage collection and a love for good finds into a business. We wanted to pour out ourselves creatively because we knew we needed something to bring us out of our darkness. Over a year into our business, we have found that we have a true love for weddings and seeing big dreams and visions come to life through our pieces. Our passion for people and our community was just the cherry on top, and we have met so many amazing people. We could not be more thankful for our business and the platform it provides to share our story of hope with so many other women during the most exciting time of their life, their wedding day. We believe that even in the midst of the darkest season, there can still be so much good. We are so excited about this next chapter as we launch our website and look forward to seeing where this business takes us. However, most of all, we just want to love people well and continue our Father's legacy of sharing hope with everyone we come in contact with and in every way we can.

www.greenhousepickersisters.com
www.facebook.com/
GreenhousePickerSisters

HEATHER GALLAGHER

My Miracle

My story is nothing new. Your young and you get married. Your next goal is to have a baby. You long to hear those life changing words you're pregnant, congrats! When those words are said your life does change. You go buy all the fun clothes and toys. Get ready to be parents and you think all is going well. Why wouldn't it? It did for your parents and their parents. Why wouldn't it go the same for you?

We had been married about 10 months and we had talked and both wanted a baby. So the fun begins. You start trying and talking about the baby as if it is here. Time goes by a bit and no such luck. I was feeling a bit under the weather and thought maybe I was going to be pregnant. Went to the store and got a test and it came back negative. I was crushed. Time went on a bit and I took another test. I was still not doing so well and it was another negative one. Then my cycle came and I was crushed.

I had been busy the next few months and lots of stress in our lives. People were sick and I was trying to take care of them. I was losing weight and feeling really under the weather. Went to the doctor to see what was wrong and he comes in and says, well congrats you are pregnant! I said "What?? No I am still having my cycle and there is no way?" He told me that this happens from time to time and nothing to be alarmed about. Scheduled me for an Ultrasound just to see what was going on. A week later, found out I was four months along. It is here and real now. Once the initial shock wore off we were so excited.

Four months along and time is flying by with so much to do and get ready for. I was still busy with family things and time was not on my side. The doctor wanted to see me once a month to make sure things were still good. The only problem I was having was that I was losing weight. I didn't seem to mind that part. I looked great at 6 months along. People thought I was lying when I told them I was having a baby.

Around 6 1/2 months I got out of the car and felt like I had wet myself. I told my husband hurry up and unlock the door. I was so embarrassed. I ran inside and grabbed a clean pair of pants and went to the restroom. When I took off my pants it was not urine it was blood and a lot of it. I called to my husband and he saw, grabbed the phone, and called the ambulance. They rushed me to the hospital and I was losing my baby. They got the bleeding to stop but, I was having contractions way too early. They put me on bed rest and some meds and a blood pressure monitor. I had to be like this till the baby was born. Life just got real again for us.

This life was not easy for either of us. The meds made me shake so bad I needed help showering and when I did get up to go to the restroom, I had to use the furniture to walk because it made me so weak. Things were going well. I did my monitor system 3 times a day and stayed on the couch till bed. Did this for a month and then things had gotten even more real.

I had been having pain in my back for a day and the doctor was not worried about it. He said it was normal and not to worry. On June 28th in the middle of the night I was in such pain I couldn't sit, lay, or walk without crying and then my side was like someone was stabbing me. My doctor's appointment was in the morning so I just rode it out. My blood pressure was up and had a few more contractions as well. Went to the doctor and he sent me to the hospital. They said I was not doing things right and that I was going to lose this baby if I didn't take better care of myself. I was at a loss because I was not doing anything wrong. I was taking my meds, monitor at the same time every day and not doing anything. So he decided to fly me to another hospital because I was to be there for the next two months waiting to have the baby. We were shocked. However not as shocked as to what was going to come.

Told my husband to come down later tomorrow when he got off of work. All they are going to do is prick me with needles and get me comfy and you need your sleep. The doctor agreed.

They started wheeling me to the helicopter and I was so scared. I had never flown before and it was a stormy night. I remember looking up at the med flight man and asked him to hit me so I wouldn't remember the flight. They were so nice and said not to worry.

The worry came when I got to Peoria IL, St. Francis Hospital. I arrived and they started pricking me with needles and doing all kinds of tests. I was in and out of consciousness and not really sure what was going on. The Doctor came in and talked with me. My life was changing and very quickly. He said "Heather, you are going to have this baby tonight. You are sick. Your body is shutting down and if you don't have the baby you will die. You still may die because your body is in bad shape but, I am going to do everything I can to save you." I responded with "What about the baby?" He said "The baby will be taken care of and it really does not matter if you die then, so will the baby no matter what. The baby will be just fine. You are the one sick." "What about my husband. He is not here and I don't think he is coming. We live two hours away." He said we have one hour at the most. We have no choice but to deliver the baby." He paused as I cried and then asked if I would like to talk with anyone? "Yes please." I responded.

He left the room and I just started to pray. How could this happen when we did everything we were supposed to. As I lay praying and crying the door opened again and it was another doctor. He explained a bit more what was happening with my body. "You have what we call the HELP Syndrome. Your body starts rejecting the baby and it starts shutting down. Your liver, kidney, and blood pressure is out of control. By delivering the baby, your body will go back to normal. The baby is doing well and looks good on all counts. He can be born. We have a top notch neonatal unit and your baby will make it." He was very reassuring and I was scared but, felt a lot better knowing more of what was going on. The door opened again and it was a priest. He talked with me and prayed. He held my hand and said he would stay with me till they took me to surgery.

This point in my life I was surprisingly calm and okay with the fact I may not make it. I wanted my son to live but, I was okay if I went. I felt very safe and secure. For some reason I knew I would see my baby boy no matter what happened. It was out of my hands and in God's hands and the doctors. We prayed again and the door opened and it was the team for the delivery room. They moved me to another bed and started rolling me down the hallway.

All of a sudden I heard my husband yelling "Heather Heather!" I said "Stop it is my husband." I told him" Bob, I am going to have the baby now and it is all okay. When he is born you go with him and take care of Austin Paul. He is going to need you with him. I love you and I am okay." He responded with "I don't understand. I love you too." The nurse came over and took his arm and explained what was going on as they wheeled me into the operating room. They started hooking me up to all kinds of things and prepping me for surgery. The last thing I remember is someone saying "Doctor....she is going to stroke out."

The next three days I was pretty much out of it. People were in and out of my room doing things to me and I had no clue of any of it. I was not clotting so they had to do platelet transfusions and blood transfusions on me. On the third day I became aware of things. The doctors came in and talked with me. "Heather you have been through a lot the past few days. We almost lost you but, you came through. You have had a blood transfusion and three platelet transfusions. Your body is healing up nicely now and you are doing great." "How is my baby?" I asked. "Your baby is doing wonderful." They said. "I want to see him please." They said maybe tomorrow.   You can't do too much today. You are just now with us and we have to build your strength up." I started to cry again. Why won't they let me see him? Is he really okay? What is wrong that I can't see him? This is what kept going on in my head. Then someone came to the door and I said no I didn't want to see anyone. Bob had gone home to go to work. I didn't care about anyone at this point but, my baby. I told the nurse please tell them I am sleeping and I am sorry. She then responded with, " you will want to see this guest." The door opened and they rolled a cart in to my bed and there was this perfect little angel in the iceolet. He was so sweet and little. She said mommy this is your baby boy Austin Paul Gallagher born at 2lbs 14 oz and fully developed just needs to grow." I of course started to cry again as she handed this perfect bundle of joy to me. He opened his eyes and I was in love. He gave me a smile even though I know they can't tell at that age but, there was a little smile. He changed my life in so many ways. More so he gave me my new life.

Austin Paul Gallagher born on June 30th at 1:15 am 2lbs 14 oz 15inches long. He had to stay in the hospital for a month to grow and get stronger and came home at 4lbs 4oz. He was perfect. He is now a 22 year old man that I am so very proud of and love more and more every day. Thank you God for our little miracle. I gave him life as much as he gave me life. I love you Austin.

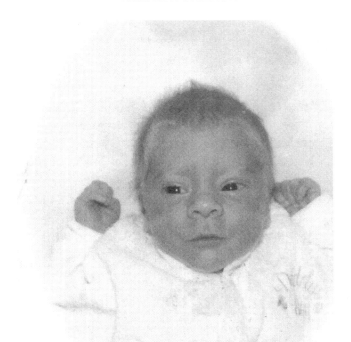

Austin Pa.. Gallagher
June 30, 1993   . Lbs. 1. Oz.

JACIE BOYD

My Thirteenth Birthday

I take a deep breath as I push open the front door to my grandparents' home. The air so thick with tension that it's nearly palpable. Today is not a day of celebrations. No. No presents, no balloons or cake. Today is the day I hoped would never come. Yet here I am.

My mom and the other adults are gathered in the kitchen speaking quietly to one another as if there were some grand secret I wasn't let in on.

"Mom" I spoke inquisitively as I enter the kitchen which is filled with the aroma of coffee. "Hey, hun". She has tears in her eyes. She has remained so strong, showing me how it's done, I followed her lead and we haven't shed one tear at the possibility.

Honestly, I believe if I don't acknowledge it, it wouldn't be true. But true it is. My superman is going to leave me. The man who has taken the place of a drug addicted absent father. The only man who has instilled any self-worth in me. The only man to show me how I should be treated by a man. The man who sees more in me than I ever thought possible. The man who helps plan my future and pushes me toward academic success. With him by my side, I am confident and powerful. My grandpa is dying and even though I know this I still can't cry because crying makes it real.

My mom grabs me and releases all the tears she has held for so long now. She held the tears through the diagnoses. She held the tears through radiation and chemotherapy. She even held the tears when he decided to surrender to an impending and absolute death; at this very moment, she let them all go.
"You should go talk to him," she said. "I'm scared" I reply. Superman can't die and this isn't true, this isn't real.

I question my mother about his consciousness to which she explains that he hasn't really been awake for two days. "They're keeping him comfortable," she says it as if it were any comfort to me.

The journey down the hall to his bedroom felt eternal and motionless all at the same time. I can hear the gurgle in his fluid filled lungs with every short, pain-filled gasp of life he takes. The beep from the monitors are a low tone in the background continuously beating the rhythm of a chant to call upon the reaper. He's so pale and yellowed. Cold. I've never seen anybody so vulnerable, helpless. Heroes can't be helpless. I hold his hand and ask him to leave. "You don't have to suffer anymore grandpa. You can go. I'll be okay, we'll all be okay." Sitting in the cold, hard plastic chair next to his hospital type hospice bed, I lay my head on our clasped hands." I love you so much grandpa". For the first time since the beginning of the end, I feel at peace. My eyes are so heavy they just close.

My eyelids begin to flutter letting in daylight. It's tomorrow. I acclimate myself to my new surroundings. I realize I'm in my grandpa's favorite overstuffed chair. Oh, it's so comfy and the smell, old spice. For a moment, I allow myself to forget until I notice the commotion coming from his room. "No" I barely manage to squeak out. Where is everyone? The beep is no longer chanting. There are no more painful gasps. The familiar sound of a zipper echoes through the house like the bang of a judge's gavel dismissing court. It's over.

"He wanted you to have this. "The trinket dangling from my mother's fingertips. His beautiful eagle charm and chain. I reach to receive my final gift from my grandpa. The gold is shiny, heavy and cold. I close my hands around it and pull it to my chest, trying to absorb his life essences from this talisman. Today, March 4, 1996, is my thirteenth birthday

and the day my hero died.

JEANNE BUESSER

To my surprise, my middle son Adam, freely chose to do a very inspirational event at 14 years old. He volunteered to do a Bar Mitzvah.

What made this so extraordinary was that Adam has significant speech and learning disorders. New words were hard for him to learn by sight. He struggled with reading. Yet, he was able to learn and speak an English translation of the Hebrew prayers. He diligently studied for many, many hours over a full years' time in order to succeed at this.

He never gave up. I was so proud of my son when I witnessed the Bar Mitzvah. I could hardly believe he was standing up in front on the Bima, the front platform in the synagogue. He was in all of his glory. I was smiling from ear to ear. His father, who had a catholic background, always seemed more comfortable with the Jewish tradition. Even though he was fairly silent during this ceremony, I just knew how much this meant to him.

Even before Adam became the first member of our family to receive this sacred ceremony, I had great intentions to do my Bar Mitzvah. It was on my bucket list, but he beat me to it.

It's only recently that I've been re-inspired to complete this celebration for myself. This was always something that I was intimidated by. It seemed out of my reach.

I went through a very dark and painful period in my life that lasted many years. It was brought on by the loss of my husband and my oldest son. In my heart, I saw them both being an intrical part of the ceremony. I had to do enormous healing, grieving, and recovery work before I could proceed. It's only recently, that I've felt strong enough to succeed. I am now ready to learn the Hebrew and Aramaic language.

Being the head of the family, I feel this is a very important passage for me and for my whole family. Josh, my youngest son also wanted the opportunity to continue the family tradition of receiving the Bar Mitzvah. Josh struggles with speaking due to autism. His schools' speech therapist volunteered to help out using a slowed down version of the Hebrew prayers. At home, he received reinforcement through a behavioral therapist. He was very committed to this. It started to feel very important to me to find a way to include my son Danny who had passed 19 years previously at 3 1/2 years old. I had always heard about the story of Daniel and the lion's den, but didn't know what it was about. I thought it was a simple story about Daniel killing a lion, but it wasn't. It was about Daniel, his faith in God, and how it protected him from the lions. In honor of Danny, I wanted to include something from this story in my Bar Mitzvah. I wanted to either read the story or sing a verse from it.

Many people study Hebrew at a much younger age than I am now. This is a very big challenge for me. I asked my rabbi about including this section from the story of Daniel. It meant so much to my heart to have Danny included through this sharing. The Rabbi had to think about it. 'This isn't part of the torah he said, but maybe you could learn to sing this in Aramaic ' which is different than Hebrew in its pronunciation.

I am glad that I am able to honor my son Daniel, with his own Bar Mitzvah passage, which he never got to do. It feels more like a shared family celebration now with all my sons included. In my faith, I remember him as the brave, courageous young man, who in spirit is with his family now and always.

Jeanne Buesser
Author, Poet, He Talks Funny, Journey From Darkness To Light, Moonlight Till Dawn, Water Line and Willow Tree coming soon!
www.jeannebuesser.com
www.health.groups.yahoo.com/group/ApraxiaNetwork/"

JENNIFER S GOLUBICH

On August 3, 2011, before 9:00 AM, my sister called me again; this time to tell me our mom's battle with Cancer had finally ended. "She pointed to the television, I think to distract us, we looked back at her and she was gone."

I was at work, my job of three years in the midst of a project. I sat down, told my sister I will call her back after I tell my supervisor I was leaving for the week. We hung up and I don't even remember breathing. I was hugged many times by coworkers before I left. I made a few calls on my cell phone before I even got to the car. I knew I was going to be away for a while, so in my overloaded head of chaos and emotions, I was trying to think of everything I had to do before I left town.

Losing my mother three years after my father's unexpected death, many things had now become a reality. No living parents made me an adult orphan. I felt very abandoned. I went home every weekend to Cleveland to see her, now those visits were over and so was my reason to go to Cleveland. So much was going to change, even the ownership of the only home I knew my whole childhood. The ones, who surrounded me with love in such a beautiful home, including my grandmother, were all reunited without me.

I was living in Columbus, Ohio at the time of Mom's passing, and drove to my sister's home in Sheffield, Ohio, a suburb outside of Cleveland. I arrived there before dark, with hopefully everything I needed for my extended stay. I had no idea how I got there, the drive was a blur to me. I remember as I was driving, how the sunset had caught my peripheral vision. I managed at one time to snap a picture of it quickly. The sunset passing me by and as beautiful as it was, reminded me of my mom's quick battle with cancer and her beautiful soul crossing over. The blurry vision of course, was caused my tearful drive.

My sister and I pulled it all together to have her visiting hours and memorial service soon after. It was odd doing this all for her, when she always was the one in the family who did what was needed, for everyone. There was a day; after all was said and done that this feeling of relief overcame me. My sister was driving, the sun was warm in her van, and I discovered my chest wasn't feeling heavy anymore. Inner warmth just filled me. To me, I could only explain it was my mother letting me know, she was OK and she wanted me to be, too. I haven't experienced that again since that day. It was an undeniable memorable experience, which I haven't spoken about until now.

In 2012, a year later, I took on the milestone of entering an online Master program in Humanities. I recalled a conversation with my mother and how she encouraged me to go back to school, but this time for writing. The concentration for my program was creating writing. During my schooling I dealt with the deepest dark moments of grief. I was even hospitalized for a week with pneumonia. My courses were almost as therapeutic as my grief group sessions. In the final capstone course, I completed a 101 page research paper on how using art expression through my grief journey saved me. It was backed by known results, including my own. Poems I wrote, photographs I took, watercolor paintings and even a short screen play I created, graced the pages of this final mammoth project required to complete the program. On May 3rd, 2014, I graduated. My husband, daughter, and step son joined me. I knew that my mother and father were there in spirit. I beamed that day.

From that moment on, I was driven to share what I learned with others. A year later I launched a Facebook closed grief group titled, Deep Grief Great Love Gallery of Healing. It started small, on Mother's Day, to honor my mother. Group members are encouraged to share about their great loves, with no criticism, no comparing to face, just validation and care would evolve for them. Today there are about 600 plus members, which more than a handful I consider like family. They respond to a daily prompt I post every morning before I get on with my day or just post independently what is on their minds, with comments of support to flood their after thoughts. I also added an open group to Facebook, where I share more pictured quotes on grief where an open forum of followers can share and comment on. Many members come from the open group to the closed

group, for they appreciate the private sharing. In the open group I share my published blog, which contains more details of my grief journey. My inbox fills daily with random messages of praise for finding a group they have discovered comfort in to cries for help as they try to learn to cope with their loss.

It is overwhelming some days to keep up with my groups and the members. Not because of the quantity of members, but because of the variety of deep emotions revealed. The testimonials of loss, from murder to still born deaths, are powerful. If I hadn't founded my groups, I would have never known the spectrum of losses and their impact on others' lives. I now realize that all losses are important and incomparable. The foundation of every deep grief journey is great love. People die, but dealing with the love lost lives on. Grief support is out there and no one needs to be on their journey alone. I was once alone, but by now reaching out, I am surrounded with many, helping them heal as they help me.

JOE SUBLER

On a Sunday afternoon in May, 2013 my wife picked up the phone and heard our horse trainer, Tammy Hawkey, on the other end saying "Get over here fast. Saffire is having her foal!" We drove to Tammy's barn as quickly as possible but missed the birth by just a few moments. A beautiful, bay Arabian colt was already making his first attempts at standing. I watched him as he stood up and took his first step and knew that a lifelong dream of mine had finally come true. This moment changed my life in ways I have difficulty explaining and only another horseperson could understand.

This story started when I was just a child. We never owned horses as I was growing up, but there were horses in the field behind our house and my mother said she had to constantly watch me to be certain I didn't run into the pasture with the horses. I was only about 3 years old at that time, but I can still remember my mother giving me sugar cubes and walking out with me to watch over me as I gave the cubes to the horses. I thought I was in heaven and can remember it as if it were yesterday. As I grew older neighbors around me would allow me to ride their ponies and horses. Then, as a teenager, I saw a picture of an Arabian horse in a magazine and thought this may be the most beautiful horse I had ever seen. I promised myself that I would someday raise my own Arabian.

As I grew older I graduated high school, went to business school then started working. I met the most beautiful woman who later became my wife and has supported me throughout the years in good times and bad but, through it all, I always prayed and dreamed that someday I would raise an Arabian horse. It seemed my dream would never come true as we were transferred from Ohio to Texas to Illinois and back to Ohio as I focused on God, family, and work. There was just never enough time to own a farm and I didn't think that owning a horse would be affordable to us since we lived in an urban setting. However, my dream of raising an Arabian horse seemed to haunt me every time we drove through the country or every time I would see someone riding a horse. I just couldn't shake that dream!

In 2004 a friend and I visited his son's farm and he had horses. His son got the horses saddled up and we rode for a few hours and I knew then that I had to do whatever it took to be able to own a horse. On my return home I discussed this with my wife and she thought I was crazy but said she would back me in whatever I chose. I thought and prayed about this until May of 2007 and decided to contact trainers to see about taking riding lessons. I looked until I found the names of 3 trainers who specialized in Arabian and Half Arabian horses and left messages with each asking for information on taking riding lessons. I had decided whomever contacted me first would be the person with whom I would take riding lessons. Tammy Hawkey was the first and only person to contact me so we made an appointment to take a riding lesson the next weekend. As my wife and I pulled onto the barn's parking lot I got out of the car and breathed in the smell of fresh cut hay and horses and I told my wife I had just died and gone to heaven as any horseperson knows! Introductions were made and Tammy went through all the safety requirements and we saddled up a purebred mare named Raisa and I stepped into the saddle. Look at me, I am sitting in a saddle on an Arabian horse and I felt like a king! We rode for approximately an hour and when I stepped out of the saddle I finally remembered that, at age 56, this wasn't going to be as easy as I thought. My knees buckled and I thought I would hit the ground but I managed to stay afoot and knew I had to continue. Tammy told us about a show that would soon be coming up so my wife and I decided to go and I was hooked after that. We saw classes of Arabian and Half Arabian horses being ridden as Park, English Pleasure, Country English, Hunt, Western and loved every moment.

I continued taking riding lessons until November, 2008 when I purchased my first Arabian. She is a purebred mare named Saffire whom both my wife and I fell in love with from the moment we met her and Tammy agreed to keep her at her barn for me and I could continue taking lessons and also take her to shows. It was amazing how many friendly and helpful people were at the barn and shows we attended. They have become my second family. However, I still had the dream that one day I would raise my own Arabian horse so in late 2011 I began to think that Saffire could give me that foal. I stayed up long hours going through information about stallions and finally decided on a stallion named Navajo Moun who was right down the road from Tammy's barn. In March of 2012 we loaded Saffire into the trailer and took her to the farm to be with Navajo Moun and in June of 2012 we knew Saffire was going to have a baby. I could not contain my happiness and prayed for a healthy baby. The long months ahead were worrisome to say the least but my prayers were answered and that brings us back to the where I began this story. Watching this beautiful little colt take it's first steps.

I picked the name of Living on a Prayer for his registration because of all the prayers that had been said. As word of his birth went out I could not believe the number of people who came to see him that day and how many calls I received. On that day I understood how much this little guy and his mother had done for us. They have given friends, literally from around the country, that I would never have known otherwise, friends who would do anything to help me. These friends have answered my never ending questions from that day to this, they have helped with smiles and tears. They are true friends. Living on a Prayer (we call him Tommy in the barn) is now a 3 year old and has just begun his training under saddle so that he can become whatever he is destined to become. But to this day, when I gaze into his eye, I remember how he changed my life in a moment of time and just how blessed we are.

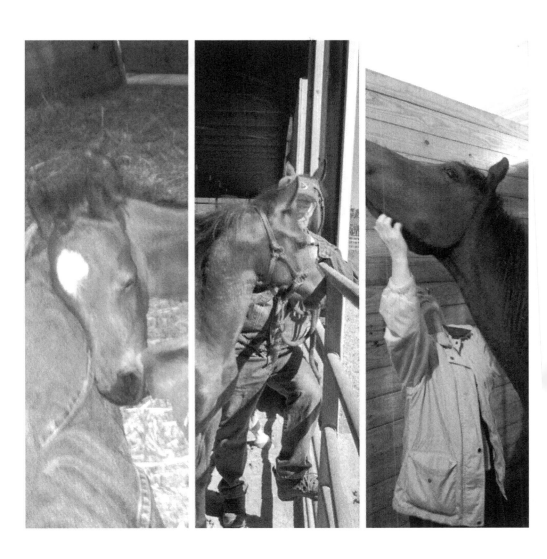

JOHN O'BRIEN

Dec. 18, 2010

The day life as I knew it, changed with just three words. Kelly has leukemia. Just hearing those words sent so many things through me. Fear, sadness, anxiety, the unknown. I couldn't catch my breath. This trap door just opened up, and I began a free-fall, all the while, an unbearable weight on my chest.

There we were, at Albany Med. Dr. Pearce gave us the tragic news. How many times had she said those same words to another family? Her words were honest, blunt, to the point. But with a hint of a smile, she told us to be hopeful, that we would be in good hands. Days later Kelly had her spleen and gall bladder removed. We spent Christmas Eve in the ICU and then Dec. 26 started the first of several chemotherapy treatments.

It seems like just days later, Kelly's hair started to fall out. Dr. Pearce convinced Kelly to shave her head before the chemo took it. I used to wash her hair, blow dry, brush, pig tail and braid those beautiful blond locks. The day Abby came, I smile and took off for coffee, so sad and hurt knowing this 16 year-old beautiful young woman would no longer have her hair. When I got back, her hair was on the floor. Kelly was still beautiful, so beautiful. I put her hair in a bag, told her I would put it with her baby teeth, and walked out for something to eat. There was a restroom in the hall. When I got there I held that bag close to me and cried like I never had.

The road trip, as Dr. Pearce called it, was very long and very hard. Very sick child, lack of sleep, every side effect ever expected. My head went to very dark, very horrific, very cold places. No one should ever have to go there. Tears kept coming, but I tried real hard not to let Kelly see. Whatever I felt paled in comparison to what Kelly was feeling or going through. My baby girl was so sick and I couldn't fix it.

Months later, after many rounds of chemo, infections, problems and issues, Kelly fought back. Dr. Pearce, her team, the oncologists, x-ray techs, nurses, they saved Kelly. Days are now brighter and I tend to be so much more aware of this disease. We give back what we can, whenever we can. We smile more, enjoy life more and tend not to take things for granted.

I remember the "Serenity Prayer" making sense one day. Perhaps it was one of the times I was in the chapel, praying to have this disease given to me, praying to make Kelly healthy, praying to have her back. So I accepted certain things, somehow. Because of Kelly, I found courage. And as far as wisdom? Well...

"Footprints in the Sand," I rewrote that in my head. Instead of one set of footprints, there were hundreds of footprints, of all who carried us through on this journey, all while God looked down from above. Perhaps that may be offensive, but that's what I believe.

So now it's five years later. Kelly is healthy, living life, ready to take on the world. Life is good.

To Albany Med, the staff, everyone involved, and of course, Dr. Pearce: Thank you for giving Kelly back to me.

To Kelly. Love, Me

Albany Medical Center
"Dancing in the Woods" 2011
Gala Video
https://vimeo.com/33984649

Kelly O'Brien story on
YouTube
www.youtube.com/
watch?v=KhPW9XpJ0UM

KATE KEESEE

And it is your freedom when you can bare your soul......hide behind nothing.…... unveiled and transparent.

What say you beautiful woman with a voice all of her own?

My journey with Salvage Dior began in 2009. It was the brainchild blog name included of my dear friend Jo Lee Vaughn. She encouraged me to share my passion for DIY and a place where a writer can unfold her story. It was just the beginning, for the trial under the fire that would shape me into a greater woman.

I hit the ground running with my blog and began to connect with the hearts of other women, and still yet not realizing my voice would later become a platform for their own pain.

I had been enjoying a very successful twenty year career of being a wedding planner and life was moving at such a fast pace until that moment of impact. That defining moment that changed the life I had always known.

In 2010 I heard the words.......Systemic Lupus in the doctor's office as my entire body went numb. As I walked out with ERH wobbly legs and a pounding heart, the doctor said that my mind would be the greatest battlefield and sharpest weapon against this disease. Those words would soon resonant the best advice above all. I stood on the solid ground of my faith, praying for grace over my emotions and a strength of vulnerability for all to see.

As the weeks and months transpired, I became more transparent and as time went on, this illness stole, like a thief in the night, the woman I once knew. Loss came knocking at my doorstep more than I was willing to admit, and I began to bloom through this adversity.

I watched myself change to the point of no return. Through moments of grief, I said good bye and then welcomed the woman that found her greatness. I was created to do many wonderful things. My heart was on fire and burning like a blaze for every woman out there who was suffering in her life. I wanted to jump in the ocean and dog paddle with them till they reached the shore. Again this illness became my greatest gift as I tossed my seduced illusions of perfect days, and lived for the glory of each moment that I was alive.

Nothing would take me prisoner. Nothing would hold me captive, and I sure was not going to let this beast of sickness define me.

I vowed that nothing would stand in the way of my greatness. There is no perfect life. We are all broken in one way or another. I stand on the battlefield of my victory. Proud of everything that I have faced head on even if I did it crawling on my belly kicking and screaming.

I have learned to love myself with a fierceness that took hold of my mind, body, and soul to the rightful place of peace where all fear ends.

True soul equals you

When I go back to think about how this illness has changed my life, it has shaped my heart beyond its former recognition.

I am now a woman who can love without question. I have seen broken, that some may not be able to bare. Blindness takes over and my soul becomes a beacon to soothe the hurting soul of another in their darkness.

Peace like a river, I have let go of the once was... my days of being healthy are long gone. I have grieved many days of who I was and who I will never be again. Every ounce of what now remains in me is the beautiful story of my soul. My pages have been dog eared, torn, some have fallen out, but it is still my story.

It's my victory as I walk upon my field of freedom. My trials have become my sword of truth. Not everything or everyone will happen the way that I had hoped for in my life. But I have found my voice and my faith that has dared my soul to go further than it can see.

To go the farthest and let my light shine bright. So bright that it even blinds my eyes to any fear that might hold me captive once more.

There was a time when I did not count a moment when I never really mattered. Nothing happened. Nothing within me and my old life felt good. I had every inch of that woman prior to Lupus memorized and scripted to a T. Unchanged, untouched, unwilling.

Nothing is more profound that the transformation that awakens your soul and screams with a loud bellowing thunder "I am here." To embrace the woman I am now was like embracing a long lost love. It became a unity of my inner voice and strength as one bond. Oh how you have taught me the real meaning of each day. It is a gift and to live fully present with no wasted thoughts on I will get to it another day. I live with a new set of eyes since an unhealthy body keeps me from a destiny as the one I had wished for inside of my heart.

You are so invisible to others as most auto immune illness are. Yet each day you are completely visible to me. Days I welcome you, and others I shut the door knowing you will never define me or break me from the joy of my soul and the positive presence that I chose for truly living.

You will walk behind me all of my days, for the love God has placed in my heart, for my life's journey, you will not take for the win. For no matter what this illness breaks down in this body of mine, love is the journey that seals my fate.

Kate Keesee
www.facebook.com/salvagedior
www.salvagedior.com
https://www.instagram.com/salvagedior/

Photos courtesy of Frank Salas

KATHRYN ALLAIRE

July 2013
Saratoga Springs, NY
I was 25 years old.

I was offered a management role after less than 2 months with a new company. I attended college for my Bachelor's Degree in Hospitality Management. After graduating, I worked in a hotel in an entry level position. I wasn't naïve enough to believe I deserved to step right into a management role, so I understood and accepted an entry level role. However, I was made promise after promise to move up into a management role and, unfortunately, it did not happen. I struggled with the stagnancy of my career and attempted to find a new job where I could do what I had always wanted: to become a manager. In my pursuit to find a new job, I landed a part-time job in a retail store. The philosophy and the mission behind the company was positive reinforcement. There was something that drew me into the brand and even though it was not a management role, I felt hopeful. I worked at the retail store and the hotel simultaneously for two months, clocking in nearly 60 hours per week. To this day, I am not sure how I was able to function, but I made it through! For a month and a half, I gave it my all in the retail store, as I do with any job. And then, one day, my manager called me into her office and offered me a management role with the store. Relief and accomplishment washed over me. I couldn't (and didn't) contain my excitement. I immediately accepted. It was liberating for me to be in the presence of managers that saw my potential and wanted to invest in me. And it had taken less than two months! It further emphasized that this company was the one for me, because they saw my spirit, talent, and drive to succeed.

I have been able to hone my skills as a manager and excel in a company that I wholeheartedly believe in and love. It made me realize that when you are passionate about something and work incredibly hard, someone will notice and someone will believe in you.

Working for this company and getting the incredible experience I have gotten has turned me into an optimistic, respected, and grateful individual. Looking back on it, this opportunity kind of just fell into my lap. It wasn't something that I had given a lot of thought to or dreamed about. I never imagined myself in a retail environment. Despite that, this job is now very close to dream-worthy.

One of the best parts about this job is the incredible teams I have worked with. How many people can say that they work with people that feel like family? The people I have met have become life-long friends, whether we are still with the company, have moved on to new locations, or taken different ventures in our lives; I have kept in touch with most of my former and current colleagues. Although I don't see these people on a daily basis like I used to, I still feel connected to them and I still carry on the traits I have learned from them. They are always with me.

KEN CATHCART

Hello,

My name is Ken Cathcart. I am a 45 year old father of 3 and have been with my better half for 13 years now. Her name is Brandi, and I love her with all my heart alongside my children. I want to start by saying even though I am going to talk a lot about struggle, I know each of every person out there has seen struggle and heartache in their own difficult way.

Here is my story... I grew up with a very loving family in the suburbs of Pennsylvania. My father was a Marine and my mother worked for GE as well as my grandfather. At the age of 10 my parents divorced which pained me in a way that took my life on a road of rebellion and disaster. My mother was stuck by herself raising my brother who at the time was only a baby. I was 10 and I began to hang out with older kids and started not to listen to the rules any more. As time went on, I went from school to school because I could not seem to grasp the part to actually go. My mother could not handle this, and I was put into different placements throughout my early life. I went from group home to institutions and finally ended up at The Wagon Train "Vision Quest" where I spent almost 2 years traveling across country by wagon trains and sleeping in Indian Teepees and lived like a Indian. This was a great experience that I am glad till this day I did. It seemed as if things would be good for me and that I would not turn to drugs or crime at this point so I moved in with my grandparents. After a year or so of finally being home with family, I began to hang out with the kids I grew up with in between my placements. Most of these friends were partying and not really going anywhere in their lives which made for a bad choice for me to have in my new life. I began to use drugs and started partying which led me to addiction that took me to being arrested at the age of 21.

I went to jail for 3 years. This was the turning point as to my never doing drugs or getting into trouble again. It took for me to go to jail to learn this lesson. After all of this now entering the world as an adult, I now have the task of finding a job with a record. Till this day at the age of 45, it still haunts me with the struggle of not being able to get a good job. Through my life I was a pro freestyle biker, pro Skater "Skateboarder", Pro Skier, wrote poetry, and produced music for a record label. I was in search to be someone great through all my years of struggle and pain. I was in search to do something to make up for any wrongs or pain I ever inflicted upon anyone else.

Well in 2009, my grandfather passed away. He was my hero in life. My grandfather and grandmother raised me for my teen years and never turned their backs on me even through the darkest of my times. My grandfather was such an amazing man. He built the Galileo probe that went to Jupiter, he taught the blind to ski, he took part in the community to help others and he always put me at the top of the list to help get straightened out. When he passed away in 2009, I was devastated. That was a tough year for me. My son, Jacob, was born and I was out of work and could not seem to find a good job anywhere because of my background. Brandi and I had broken up at that time because I could not seem to support a family which broke my heart to the extreme along with the passing of my grandfather. I stood at his memorial with tears running down my face losing my breath with the wanting to end my life. I was feeling the end and I did not want to go on any further....

As I stood there talking to my grandfather and crying so hard I began to stare around at the other memorials around my grandfather's grounds. This is when everything changed for me... I out of nowhere came into this thought of creating a way for the grounds we all so cherish to have a more personal way to visit and a better way to make these grounds more accessible for people who move away or are disabled and cannot make it out to the grounds.... I came up with Serenity Cam and Angelbook. I stood there in disbelief that I came up with this idea, and I can only believe it was my grandfather who left this last gift to me. I was overwhelmed because I knew how big this was gonna be. It could help so many people all over to view and keep their loved memories alive and help shape the funeral industry towards technology and social media. I walked away with a whole new feeling inside, it was hope... It was the only thing at the time that kept me going enough to make this happen for my life. My grandfather and the so many people that deserve to have this tool in place for their family's grounds everywhere.

At this point, I had no idea what to do. It haunted me each and every day for the next 2 years.... I had no clue as to how to patent or come up with the money needed to fund such a big thing. I told my friend down in Mississippi, Daniel, of this idea. He agreed it was something truly amazing, so he brainstormed with me to figure it out. In 2010, Brandi and I had gotten back together. I found work to survive on for a bit. I was living in an old coal town in Pa. in a 200 year old house. On Labor Day 2010 while just awakening in the house with the kids, the house began to shake and began to collapse with us in it. Before we knew it, we all made it outside watching as it rained bricks and parts of walls onto the ground. The streets were covered with fire trucks, police, and news crews as we stood with the kids crying and helpless as to what now. We ended up staying in my father's RV at this point. I got laid off during this time which made it very hard to once again to deal with life. I felt such a reminder of pain and struggle once more. I finally broke down in the RV and said "That's it, I'm reaching out to my great uncle who I really don't talk to" to see if he could help with this idea of SerenityCam and Angelbook.

He emailed me back to tell him more. I did, and that was the turning point for this idea that my grandfather distilled in me that day standing at his grounds. Here we are today, I still am struggling extremely hard with my family, but we have hope for AngelBook and SerenityCam. We want it to become this amazing company that will help people across the globe view their family's grounds and bring money in to help people who suffer in natural disasters and other things that happen where life is lost. I want and hope that this company will not just be a new and innovative way to memorialize your loved ones, but to be a company that will reach out and be there for people who have been affected by a tragedy. This is only part of my story, for there is so much more that maybe someday I can, and will write about. The love I have for people and the grieving process in which I have learned a lot about, has molded me into a different person that I am today. Myself, the AngelBook team, and family all send their love and light to all who take part and those who do not. Let's better the world together one small step at a time~

For those wondering what SerenityCam is and AngelBook:
SerenityCam is the first solar powered camera system for your family's resting grounds that aims at the memorial and gives you a view of it at any moment. It's connected back to a social network called Angelbook.com. Here you can view it and the tribute you have made for the person you have it set up for. Angelbook will provide a way to customize a memorial or tribute for each and every person that has passed in your life. This will keep their legacy alive and fresh in the digital age we live. As the user of this page, you create your own profile in which you will record your life events so that someday

you will have created your own story and tribute that your family can add to and so on and so on...

Ken Cathcart
Www.facebook.com/angelbookworldwide
Twitter name is @MyAngelbook
Instagram is famous_angels

Larissa Haynes

I grew up in a large family with brothers and a sister, and parents who truly did everything in their power to give me all that I ever needed and more. My childhood home was a dream home in many instances with a landscape and amenities that most dream of. Would I call myself blessed? Absolutely. Though, at times, it would seem something was missing. It wasn't until I was 18 years old that I chose to take a step that would change my life forever.

You see, I made a decision to place the Lord Jesus Christ first and foremost, and coming from a young girl that thoroughly was enjoying her teenage years with all that it has to offer, this was a turning point of enormous proportions. When some come to Christ they slowly lean into it, but for me it was all or nothing. I threw away books, music, clothing, changed my language, and even my attitude towards my family. Everything became new and I felt like an elephant had been lifted from my back. In that one second, I was free.

From there, I also made life decisions that took me to a Bible college where I graduated with honors and earned my bachelor's degree in Interpersonal & Organizational Communication with a minor in Business Administration. Primarily, my degree would have set me up to be a business consultant, but becoming a wife and mother was more important to me. I married my high school sweetheart during our junior year of college and was the best thing I could have ever done. He was integral in my becoming a Christian, and also my best friend.

Shortly after graduating college, my husband and I began our adventure as parents while focusing on his higher education. I became a stay-at-home mother and eventually had five children. Talk about the second your life will change forever! I had some difficulties during my pregnancies, one of which is where I contracted pneumonia. I became horribly sick with a staph blood infection that caused me to be in the intensive care unit for eleven days while pregnant with my second child. In that time I knew what it felt like to suffocate and panicked with a fear I had never felt before. During that illness, I also had an episode where they thought I was dying. My blood pressure dropped and I went out like a light. This happened on the first night my husband I had ever been apart since being married because I sent him home to be with our one year old son, while my father stayed with me. I woke up to find numerous people hovering over me and anxiously skittering about. They asked me to tell them where I was and I wondered, "Duh, I'm in the hospital." I had no idea what had happened, but my recovery back to breathing was a difficult one. You can bet I had a new outlook on life after that.

My next few pregnancies had complications with a bleeding between my uterine wall and the embryonic sac called a subchorionic hematoma. It didn't affect my next three children and their deliveries, but it did with my sixth pregnancy which caused us to have a stillborn daughter at 21 weeks gestation. I have always said that no one should have to bear the grief of losing and burying a child. With much sadness, our next child would also be taken to the Lord too early. My heart was broken to pieces after the loss of two children, but I knew God was in control.

There was a span of about three years in my life when I did not become pregnant after that, and I went from either being pregnant or nursing for ten years to not knowing what to do with myself. My husband and I believe in letting God choose the size of your family and I feel He knew I needed time to heal in more ways than one. It was in this time that I made some major dietary changes and I started to work on furniture to earn extra income. Not long after, I opened up a business, and felt the desire to create a blog where I could share my ideas and inspire others to create for themselves. This is coming from a lady who could have lived happily ever after without a computer, without social media, and lived off the grid. I still could.

When I became pregnant with my eighth pregnancy, I was scared and praying that our baby would be the healing balm I needed. Some would say that I shouldn't have had such sadness as I already had five children. Those people never lost a baby. With much trepidation on my part, our daughter decided to enter the world six weeks early, which gave us an extended stay in the neonatal intensive care unit (NICU) in the same hospital I kissed our tiny baby goodbye. Those were the hardest days ever for me because I never left the hospital for three weeks. I missed my children, my home, and was used to giving birth to my babies at home. My world was upside down...but I had our daughter, my family, and my Lord.

Now, I am currently homeschooling our six wonderful children while maintaining my business that has shipped all over the globe, and creatively writing for my blog which has led to magazine features and getting to know a wonderful array of people. Would I have thought my decision to follow the Lord would take me on such a journey? No, but I wouldn't have changed it for the world. Each experience has stretched me and caused me to grow in ways that has made me strong and understand the true importance of life and our time on this earth. Now I can truly say I am blessed.

Prodigal Pieces
prodigalpieces.com
prodigalpieces.etsy.com

MARY CALHOUN

My daddy had just moved into a house with me so that I could be his guardian and caregiver. He would be closer to the hospitals and doctors. He would be safer than the house where I grew up for the neighborhood there was filled with crime. He could rest easier and I would be more at peace. And my brother, who had been his housemate, could finally have a life of his own.

I was at work the day my daddy called me to inform me my brother was having surgery to remove a kidney stone. It just wouldn't pass and the pain was growing more and more intense. So the next day we both waited while the surgeons went in and removed the stone.

As we waited for the results in his room, my brother was his jovial self as ever. I can still hear his ear piercing laughter.

"Mr. Calhoun?" said the doctor, "I have your test results. We removed the kidney stone, but when we opened you up, we found something else. We found cancer and it has spread. We are sending you to a local Oncologist for treatment."

CANCER......the word rang in all of our ears. Not what we were expecting. We were numb. Shocked. So stunned we didn't know what to do, what to think.

After a few days of letting the news sink in, my brother was sent home to recover. I insisted he come home with me and my daddy. He saw the Oncologist a few days later, but wouldn't tell us what he said. He did decide to go to Houston Clinic in Houston, TX for treatment. At least he was deciding to fight and that is what we all wanted.

In the meantime, I juggled caring for my daddy and working full time. My brother went to Houston Clinic for experimental treatments. The second trip out, I went with him because the treatments required someone to watch over him. After that trip, treatments were transferred back to our local hospital.

At that point, I moved him in with us. My daddy, who suffered from emphysema, used an oxygen machine. My brother was also given an oxygen machine so caring for two people and working full time became a more difficult road to travel. But I did it. Never thought twice about it. I just wanted them both to fight. We lost my mother nine years before, two days before my twenty-fourth birthday. That was a changing moment in my life. Caring for both of them at the same time and working full time became another changing moment.

The treatments grew more intense and his job allowed him to come home early when sickness overcame him. It was a Friday night and I was so exhausted. I turned in early, but woke up around 2:00 a.m. Something kept telling me to check on my brother.

I walked into his room and found him shivering and unable to talk. He had been calling for help and no one heard him. That was a defining and changing moment for me. I was devastated to know he needed me and I wasn't there. I piled blankets on him and did not leave the room until morning. That day I purchased a baby monitor and put one in his room and one in mine. He would never be more than a call away again.

By October of that year, he lost his battle with cancer at age 46. Not able to stop because I had my daddy, who had just lost a child, to care for and work to deal with. I kept going. Six months later I was diagnosed with system lupus with numbers that "shot off the chart" according to my rheumatologist. Two years after my brother died, my daddy died. I was 35 yrs. Old when I lost the last member of my family.

My brother's death was the second my life changed forever. I was ready for my mama's and daddy's deaths. But my brother was a strong man. He was older than me. He was suppose to be here. After all, my parents had me thirteen years after him so that he would not be alone in the world. It was my purpose to be there for him, but he was my protector, my rock. I was devastated. I was angry. It tore me apart.

Defining moments came with sledgehammer impacts on my life. The problem was they came so close together. I believe the hardest of those impacts has been dealing with the loss of my health alone. After my daddy died, I never married. Instead I dealt with my own impacts of hospitals, medications, treatments, struggles, etc.

As for caring for my family, I wouldn't have traded a single moment of time with any of them. And life has its struggles, but God has shown He is control and cares for every need I have. Never a day passes that I am not reminded I am still here for a reason, His reason, His enduring love and care.

MATT DINERMAN

THE PHONE CALL THAT CHANGED MY LIFE FOREVER

When a kindergarten teacher asks a student, "What do you want to do when you grow up?" that student usually does not reply, "I want to call horse races." Like everyone else in the room, my answer was probably stereotypical, something like, "I want to be a policeman." But for some good reasons, at age 11, I was interested in working in a very unique industry: thoroughbred racing.

I grew up ten minutes from the Del Mar Racetrack, one of the premier horse racetracks in the country. My dad was and still is a fan of the Sport of Kings, and was on the board of a non-profit organization called Tranquility Farm, that helps retired racehorses find new homes after their racing careers. So from the very first day he introduced me to the horse racing world, I was mesmerized, and knew it was an industry I wanted to be a part of.

At 16 I was old enough to acquire a work permit, and I was introduced by Gayle Van Leer, a bloodstock agent and family friend, to John Sadler, and I began working as a hot walker for John Sadler Racing Stables. John is one of the top trainers in Southern California, which is quite an accomplishment, considering California has some of the best racing in the country, and some of the best horsemen. I had to wake up at 4:30 AM every morning, 6 days a week, and I worked directly with the racehorses. Hands on, and I loved it, enough to go back for four summers. Then an opportunity to work in the Del Mar Press Box came up and I applied for the job without hesitation. Luckily for me, the interview went well, and I got the job. For two summers, I worked in the Press Box, under the direction of Dan Smith and Walter 'Mac' McBride, learning how the media gathers and releases information to the press, the horseman, the public, everyone really.

One day, in a conversation my dad told me that I'd always been fascinated with the track announcer, always asking questions about the announcer and how, for example, he was able to remember all the horses. The announcer at Del Mar is Trevor Denman, who is like The Vin Scully or Doc Emrick of horse racing.

During my time in The Press Box, I got a chance to meet Trevor and chat extensively. It was during that first year I developed a strong desire to try announcing, because I wanted a job at the track, where I could watch and analyze all of the races and be around horses. I received binoculars for my birthday from my Uncle Joe, and in my second year of working in The Press Box, I used them to see the horses while recording calls into my cell phone. Then I would play them back, critique myself, and work on improving my accuracy, my pace and my ability to remember silks and names. Eventually, I mustered up the courage to share my tapes with Trevor Denman, who told me I had a talent and could be a very good announcer if I kept practicing. Talk about a confidence boost! Tom Quigley, who is a handicapper, and many others, told me the same thing, and that also gave me confidence.

During my senior year at Chapman University, where I was majoring in communication studies, I continued to practice calling races at Santa Anita, where I'd been given an out of the way spot on the roof by Mike Wilman, the Director of Publicity at Santa Anita. Five weeks before my graduation, I saw a press release that Emerald Downs, a really nice racetrack near Seattle, was looking for an announcer to replace veteran, Robert Geller, who was moving to Woodbine in Toronto. The only catch was the press release invited "announcers with experience" to send their tapes and resume. I knew I did not have the experience, but I figured I should send in my tape, so people would know my name, and maybe, just maybe, I would get lucky and get a shot at it.

After sending in my tapes, I asked Trevor what he thought and he cautioned me that most tracks would not hire someone without experience over the microphone. Nonetheless, I figured it was worth a try.

Several weeks later, while driving home from Santa Anita, I got a call from Emerald Down's Vice President of Marketing, Sophia McKee. What was I doing at Santa Anita on a Friday? Practicing race calls on the roof, of course. Sophia asked me to fly up to Seattle next day and audition. I'd call two races..................... live! Immediately, my stomach began churning and my palms began to sweat. I couldn't believe what I was hearing. Within an hour, my flight and hotel reservations were planned. I didn't get much sleep that night. Maybe two hours. I was wired, to say the least.

The official day of my tryout was May 9, 2015. I was to call Races 4 and 5. On the plane ride to Seattle, I looked over the horse's names and tried to memorize them. #1 in Race 4...Clemkadiddlehopper. Lovely. That will be easy to say.

Sophia picked me up at the airport. I later learned my tapes were played for a committee and Sophia was a key person pushing to give me a shot at the job.

Sophia introduced me to many people at the track, from Phil Ziegler, the track President, and to other executives, like Ron Crockett, the track's founder, and I met some of the trainers and jockeys too. Soon, I was up on the 5th floor, spending time with Robert Geller, who was the only announcer in Emerald Downs' 20-year history. He told me that he loved my tapes and showed me how he did things. His kindness and attention made me feel more at ease and it also helped my confidence.

Before I knew it, the microphone was mine and I was about to give it my best shot. The horses came onto the track for the post parade and my palms were sweating and my hands were shaking. I looked over the horses and silks again and before I knew it, the horses were at the gate. Fortunately, for this a one-mile race, the horses were going to start right in front of us. When all the horses loaded, I said, "Six in line, we're ready to go." The gates opened, the horses were off, and I started telling the crowd what I saw. It was a minute and 36 seconds of an amazing adrenaline rush that I loved. Once the race ended, I removed my microphone, and rushed outside the announcer's booth to the patio to find Carl, the track cameraman, and Robert, who was sitting on a coach, taking in the action.

"How did I do Robert?" I asked, not having remembered a word I said.
"Oh, that was fantastic," said Robert.

Those words of encouragement carried me into the second race with more confidence, and I actually enjoyed calling it. The audition complete, I was invited to dinner that evening with several of the staff, and the next day, on Mother's Day, I was offered the job, a dream job for sure. At that point, at the ripe age of 23, I had become the youngest track announcer in the country, and got my dream job right out of college.

I like to think I had the talent to open this door, but I've had a lot of help along the way and a lot of luck too. The team at Emerald Downs has given me every opportunity to contribute to success, and in some cases, I've been asked to do things I've never done before.

I learned a lesson that dreams can be achieved. No matter how slim the chance, take a swing. Give it a try. I also learned to not be afraid to step outside my comfort zone, which has made me a stronger person, willing to take a chance.

Today, I am at Emerald Downs and announcing with a passion. I love my job, and every day I wake up excited to go to work and with an appreciation for all those who helped me. I'll never forget them and I want to do the same for others because being 'The Voice of Emerald Downs' sure does not feel like a "job." As the saying goes, "If you do something you love, you won't work a day in your life." So far, I have not worked a day in my life.

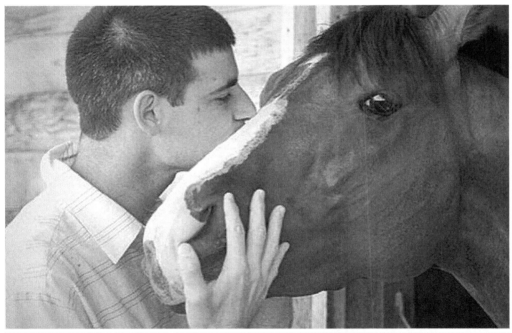

MAYA MCNULTY

It was the summer of 2012. Laying in my hammock at Sacandaga Lake, NY. Soon to be celebrating the big 40. The sun was hot. You can hear the waves softly breaking against the rocks along the beach shore. You can smell the flowers, fresh cut grass, ash burning fire pit from the night before camp fire and lake dewy freshness while being comforted by the shady trees. Calmness fans in from the soft breeze and soothing sounds of the water rolling in. Completely relaxed, and enjoying this slice of heaven in the Adirondacks. I was totally unwinding, unplugged and just relaxing from the everyday hustle and bustle from the city and virtual world daily grind. While resting in my hammock I enjoy reading and sometimes writing. I began to think of the many chapters of my life. One was closing and a new decade rapidly approaching. I decided to cracked opened a notepad and began to journal about the different lives I lived in 4 decades. Who I was. Who I became. Who I'm creating to be. Here's what I found.

Who I was: I was a woman who didn't love herself enough. I trusted people who didn't deserve my loyalty. I gave generously and without expectations. I attracted the wrong crowd who ultimately tried to ruin my life, business and family. Because I didn't love myself enough, I gave other's the power to thieve my sole and purpose.

Who I became: I became a mean woman. Bitterness fueled my emotions like a cup of bad java. Full of hate and frustration by the lack of respect, trust, friendship, and loyalty. I was being undermined, manipulated, and lied to by everyone in my tribe. I started to believe that this was my law of attraction. My self - esteem hit rock bottom as I gave my power and control away powerlessly. I was lonely, lifeless and dying inside from a lack of hope and self- love. I became depressed and felt worthless. In 2001, I had owned 2 failing franchises. The businesses struggled for over 8 long years and took a financial death plunge on our finances and marriage. Owning the franchises wasn't a mistake but a valuable lesson. I lost clients, friends, my businesses, real estate, and lots of money. The economy was tanking, people were losing jobs, their homes, and even healthcare. It was a really dark time. I didn't want this failure to become my law of attraction. By 2010, I had enough. I pulled the plug to stop the bleeding, paid thousands of dollars to franchise lawyers and closed this chapter the money pit. I needed to reinvent myself. But how? It was a difficult time. For almost 10 years my skills became obsolete and not marketable. I began searching for jobs only to learn my skill set was vintage. I was a type writer in a Mac world. I was devastated and emotional bankrupted. I lost hope, my businesses, my building, my friends, tons of money, and investments. The fights at home escalated and became emotionally crippling. You knew you had failed but being called a failure is difficult to swallow. Yes, I've been called a failure and other creative names not appropriate for publishing. These events all shaped me for the woman I am creating to be.

Who I'm creating to be: So jump ahead to summer of 2012, while swinging in the hammock, answers came to me. A vision of a one page business plan designed to assist small businesses and entrepreneurs find creative and innovative solutions to market and grow their small businesses. Since I had no luck with the job market I decided to create endless opportunities not just for myself but for many small businesses that faced the same struggles. As a joke I named my new Startup "Up IN Your Business" Marketing and Business Consultant for entrepreneurs. I reinvented myself just like that. Educated and armed with a bachelor degree in marketing I began a new journey. I boot strapped and swam in trenches to gain customer loyalty and business. I created advertising booklets to cooperatively work with universities and local businesses. I began hosting my own television show called SCENE TV, which showcases businesses and not for profits their community edge. I began hosting UPTHEBIZ monthly lunch and networking groups to share content and information to advance their businesses, and I designed a mobile app called Where to Shop and Dine. The App is a free download on Google Play Store or Apple App store. The app is a marketing tool used to promote local businesses to the best and safest experience 3-5 miles within a college region. Since 2012, the app and UPTHEBIZ lunch and networking group makes a positive financial community impact of over $15K per month. I'm a self -taught app developer, marketer, TV host and graphic designer. I created a tool that wasn't available to entrepreneurs, small businesses, colleges, and Main St. America. The loss of the franchises was a blessing. I learned that "You miss one-hundred of the shots you don't take." – Wayne Gretzky   If I hadn't gone out there and struggled trying, it was never going to happen. My journey is still full throttle ahead. I'm filled with gratitude, love, laughter and my self– esteem has been lifted. I no longer feel worthless and incompetent like some have tried to make me feel. Many entrepreneurs, business leaders, General Managers, and big businesses continually reach out seeking advice and strategic business solutions from my business coaching and advertising company. One of my favorite and best books I've ever read Think and Grow Rich by Napoleon Hill. The message of Faith, Taking Action, and Desire this triangle has become visionary and fuels my passion for success. Along the way I learned many lessons as we all do. Henry Ford said, "Whether you think you can or you think you can't, you're right." I was struggling to love myself, I gave my power away, I self -blamed. This mental abuse was a ticking bomb to the Psychiatric hospital. I fought the odds by believing that there is a better plan for me. I believed that I'm good enough. Through prayers and mediation I learned to embrace and appreciate who I was creating to be. I've learned to become a better listener, to give more that I receive. I've learned to think with an abundance mindset and to embrace changes. I've learn to meet people where they're at and not where I wanted them to be. But most of all, I learned to forgive myself and others. I'm learning to Let Go! Letting go of people and things that no longer serve me. Clarity comes from within. So embrace your best self and don't stop believing in all that is possible.

Maya McNulty, CEO and Founder
Up IN Your Business
www.upthebiz.com

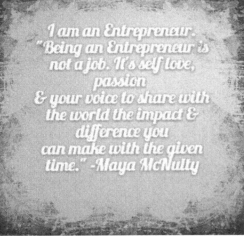

I am an Entrepreneur.
"Being an Entrepreneur is
not a job. It's self love,
passion
& your voice to share with
the world the impact &
difference you
can make with the given
time." -Maya McNulty

MELISSA CARTER

Fall, 2013
32 years old
My life changed forever when I realized my life's purpose and that my dreams are becoming a reality.

From a little girl, I always had elaborate dreams. In the Spring of 2014, I started a business, The Wholistic Package, as a Reiki practitioner. I started receiving Reiki a few years ago, as a way to add balance to my own life and reduce negativity. I soon realized that I wanted to become certified in Reiki and offer it to others as a way to help improve their wellness.

I never imagined having a wellness business, however when I realized Reiki helped me through some challenging times, I wanted to offer it to others. At the time I was also working on a children's book and that eventually came to fruition. I recently incorporated everything into one business, which now includes, Reiki, writing, , and inspirational apparel.

I have learned a vast amount of lessons, from starting a business. I have learned a lot about myself and my own strength and character. There are many successes and challenges each day. I believe that you can have it all, but it comes in stages. I also have learned that success is not universal, it is defined by you. To me, inspiring someone and having a positive impact on their life, is success. Fulfilling my passions and dreams is successful. I've learned that you have to embrace the challenges as well. You can't dwell on things that don't go as planned, you have to figure out a solution and act and be adaptable. I've learned you have to get out of your comfort zone to grow. I've learned that my message and mission are important and valuable. I've learned that true joy, comes from following your passions, whether it's a business or you are pursuing it as a hobby. I've learned that passions know no boundaries and I don't think anything is out of my reach, if I work for it. I've learned that everyone is capable of making their dreams a reality, if they work hard and persevere. I've learned to have gratitude for what I have, for all that I've accomplished and to live in the moment and enjoy those things, even the smallest accomplishments. Most important, I've learned to truly believe in myself and always be authentic.

This has shaped my life, because it allows me to follow my true passion and mission of life, which is helping others; mentally, physically, spiritually and emotionally. This experience has opened my eyes to know that I am on the path of greatness and the things that I do every day, affect people in a positive way, and that's the journey I enjoy living. This has allowed true contentment in my life, knowing that I can share my strengths, talents, challenges and learning experiences with others and pass along knowledge. I have learned that I'm always learning and having a mentor, as well as supportive people, in your life is important. I have learned that positivity is key, in all aspects of business and life. This experience allows me to smile each day and contributes to the concepts of my business, which are wellness and wholeness; defined as being content mentally, physically and spiritually.

I have learned that I am here to help others define their purpose. I have learned I'm a woman with passions, a woman with a path and a woman with a purpose and that has changed my life forever.

Little Lucky LadyBug
by Melissa Carter

One Step can make all the difference

MICHAEL CONNELL

March 27, 1969
Sears in Quincy, MA
I was 11 years old
It was my birthday, I bought a Super 8 movie camera and became an aspiring filmmaker.
I began to make films with family and friends. I started shooting all kinds of things, magic disappearing tricks, family parties, Celtics games I attended, other sporting events. I was hooked on making films.
I learned how important it is to understand something you love can be a career path, but that you need further education to make it a reality. Not everyone knows what they want to do at such a young age, so consider it a blessing. Also, your dreams may not actually be realized but you can still enjoy what you do.
I am still making films today, both professionally and for my family. I have a son in college who is not real sure about what he wants to do for a career, so I work with him to help him understand what motivates him and what makes him happy. Working a job you love is really important to life happiness.

The Second My Life Changed Forever

My name is Michael Connell and I am a video producer. I love telling stories with moving pictures, sounds, and music. I have been shooting film and movies since the day my life was changed forever, on March 27, 1969. It was my 11th birthday, and I wanted a movie camera as a gift. Since my parents had 9 children, they couldn't afford to give me such an expensive gift, so I saved up money from my daily paper routes, and combined it with money I got for gifts. I bought the Super 8 movie camera at Sears in Quincy, MA, and it was the best gift I ever got! I immediately started making movies with family and friends. My brothers and I and my best friend Eddie made funny movies in my driveway. We would do disappearing acts, great feats of jumping up on the roof of the garage, making long distance basketball shots at will. My mother thought these were the funniest films she ever watched. I was hooked.
In Junior High I made movies in class using black and white video equipment from the school media center. Since I wrote the scripts too, I can even remember lines from, "There's Rosetta on the Docks", from pre-Columbus days in Italy. Very funny today. My friends still kid me about it.

High School didn't have any media center availability to me, but I knew I was going to study film and TV. Stephen Spielberg had nothing on me. I graduated third in my class and turned down a chance to go to Harvard, because I wanted Emerson College in Boston, the best media school in the area. So Emerson is where I went for the next 4 years.

It was exciting, learning TV, radio, film, and acting. I envy the kids today. They are learning on digital cameras and computers, when I learned on gigantic old analog TV equipment. Nevertheless, telling stories with pictures works the same way today as it did then. As long as there is a good story to tell, you still need to light the pictures, record good sound, frame the content for major impact, edit with pace and style, and deliver the completed project. It doesn't matter if the final product is on reel to reel tape, cassettes, disk drives, or cell phones. The audience enjoys great visual storytelling.

My career has taken me to many places in the world, having worked first in Cable TV as a news producer, writer, reporter, and yes, even news anchor for a short bit. I even found myself at one point in a parking lot trailer, late at night, playing soft porn movies for adult cable subscribers.

In 1980, I landed a job in a world I didn't even know existed, as a corporate TV producer for an insurance company. This was far different than the Hollywood dream I had in my head, but it was a paycheck. I had to learn all aspects of commercial insurance, and learn to teach it via video, in a fun and watchable way! No easy task, but the next 8 years were awesome, traveling the U.S. and the world, shooting sales conventions in places like Rio de Janeiro, Cancun, Mexico, Montreux Switzerland and many other exotic spots in the world. I learned all about dealing with customs, including handing out bribes to clear equipment, using international carnet documents, and dealing with differences in electric power.

In 1988, the insurance company went into bankruptcy. I bought the video equipment at fire sale prices and went into my own business, KC Visuals Unlimited, Inc., where I still reside today. I have seen the journey from analog to digital through, with its fantastic new workflows, price reductions, and explosion into the wonderful wild world of the Internet. Video is used for so many things now, it is amazing.

I love my work even more today than I did when I started out. I have produced thousands of videos over the years, with a huge variety of equipment and a wide range in quality. But the basics of great storytelling are still the same…. Define your audience, analyze, and determine what makes them tick, establish goals and objectives for the video, then use great production values to tell them a story, and call them to action. Video is a must use marketing tool today, and I am in the thick of it.

So my life changed back on March 27, 1969, when I bought my first movie camera, and I've been making movies ever since. "And Loving It!" – Maxwell Smart, Agent '86

MIRANDA VONFRICKEN

Summer 2015
My backyard
I was 35
I woke up. I realized what was right in front of me.
It changed how I saw my life and all the blessings I already have. It changed how I live and how I see my future.
I learned to appreciate all that I have today. I now know that I am not a failure because I didn't accomplish my original plan but that I am quite successful for realizing what I have is so much better. I also know that God also has a plan... and his is more beautiful than ours could ever be.

Today I am still a dreamer but I don't dream alone. I have my wonderful family to dream with. I still make big plans but I know that I've already achieved more than most. By changing my mindset and truly seeing all that I already have I am able to plan better, focus harder, and act on dreams that are more me. I no longer long for a "different" life, I no longer visualize a life where I'm constantly in the spotlight. Now, I crave a deeper meaning from life and although I still sing and dance, I get just as much enjoyment from doing it in my pjs with my four year old as I do when I'm in heals and on stage.

The story
I have a very vivid memory of myself in my early 20s, standing in the kitchen of my tiny apartment. I was in the process of moving out of my own place and into an apartment with a friend. We were saving money for one year then making our way to California where I'd go to be famous and live the fabulous life. I was talented, motivated, and determined to be Brittney Spears. Ok, that role was already taken but I remember saying to myself, in a very clear moment of prayer, "I will do this. This is what I want for my life. I want my name in lights. And if it doesn't work out, I'll just come back home, get a job, get married and have kids..." I had it all planned out, my dream life and the backup plan. Little did I know, I'd never even make it to California.

I spent my high school years singing, dancing, and acting; I spent my college years doing the same. The plan was to make it big. Everyone knew I'd be "something" once I got there. As time passed my friend and I decided not to go to California. But I still had a plan. I would move to NYC and make it there. After a short period of auditions, jobs, and unfulfilled goals, I decided to move back home. Disappointed in myself, afraid of what people would say, and full of fear; what would I do now? Oh yeah… I guess I did have that backup plan, or plan "B" as I called it.

I got a job, got over my insecurities of what others thought and tried to enjoy this "backup" version of my life. Shortly after I returned home I met a young man (isn't there always a boy?) His name was Ben, I called him B for fun. I didn't realize at the time, or even after we were married and had a beautiful baby girl, that I was actually living this other plan I had for myself… my plan B. The stress of being a wife and mother sometimes gets to me. Life can be one "to-do" after the other, and I often wonder if I would have been happier just fighting a little harder for that original dream life.

Then one day, as I sat in the back yard of our new home. I saw my son and his friends jumping on the trampoline, my daughter chasing the dog, and my husband starting a fire so we could all roast marshmallows I realized… I was actually living my plan B and it was perfect!

Not only did I get a job (which I love), got married (to a fabulous man), had a baby (and a step son that I adore), I didn't just come home, I created a home. During all of this, I also found God. Finding Him and learning of His love made it all clear. This wasn't a backup plan. This WAS the plan all along.
Plan B? Sure. But it no longer stands for Backup it's for Ben, babies, beauty, and blessings. I may not be "famous" in the popular respect, but boy am I living a fabulous life… and I know the BEST is yet to come.

Monte Vacarelli

I was in my early teens when I met Nils Smiland. Nils was a retired carpenter, property investor and WWII Navy Veteran.

Nils served in the U.S. Navy from 1941-1945. He was present at the Normandy invasion June 6th, 1944. Nils served as Chief Pharmacist on the USS 488. After the war he spent the next 30 years as a carpenter and property investor. Nils passed away in early 1997. I am grateful to have had Nils as mentor in my life.

I spent many days working with and talking with Nils. He shared many stories of his upbringing during the Great Depression, and his time as a sailor. I witnessed the internal tumult he lived due to the horrific things he experienced during WWII. Nils drank and smoked heavily to try to suppress the emotional burden and it eventually cost him health.

The day my life changed was when I was in the 7th grade. We had a "book fair" at school one day and I Noticed a book titled "D-Day, June the 6th 1944". I purchased the book and couldn't wait to get home to start reading it. I read that book over the next few days. I remember staring at the pictures inside and reading the captions next to each picture. I read that book cover to cover that week and was just amazed by the story.

That following weekend I knew I was going to visit Nils and tell him about the book. I brought the book with me so that I could show it to him. While sitting at his kitchen table, Nils and I were talking about the book I had just read. He asked me if he could borrow the book overnight. I kindly obliged.

The next day, Nils and I were sitting at the kitchen table again. He looked terrible from little sleep plus drinking all night prior while reading the book. He read the whole book overnight. He thanked me for lending it to him and then proceeded to cry, sob, and moan. I could see that this was very painful for him. After a minute, he gathered his composure. He said that the book was accurate and well written. He commented on the pictures with great detail and told me how the battle took place. He broke down several times during his story. What I remember next was his long pause. He then looked right at me and said "Son, you never want to go to war. Ever!". It was at that moment when everything changed for me. My entire perspective on life had just been rocked like a hurricane! Nils had just taught me about the value of time, family, and friends. I gained incredible insight from someone who had lived a very full yet difficult life.

Nils's influence in my life has been profound. Everything he taught me continues to serve me today. Among the many lessons I learned was, how to use tools, how to take care of the tools, and most importantly, he instilled in me a solid work ethic.

While Nils' health was in decline, he maintained his investments/finances diligently and taught me how to make my money work for me verses always having to work for money.

The most important lessons that shaped my life were:
Be good for your word.
The value of time.
The true value of money.
Never give up on your dreams regardless of your circumstances.
Make the best of everything.
Take care of your tools and they will take care of you.
Learn to let go.... You can't bury the past with Alcohol and cigarettes.
Never stop learning.
My experience with Nils has made me a disciplined, diligent, orderly and successful business owner that enjoys giving back to my community through volunteering, supporting charities, and mentoring up and coming Entrepreneurs.

Pic 1 (previous page) is believed to be at Slapton Sands, England in early Spring 1942 during preparation for the D-Day invasion.
Pic 2 is the 488 unloading troops at Normandy, June 6th 1944.

PAUL RUTHERFORD

Perspective

When you travel half a world from home your awareness is always heightened. Now when you find yourself meandering in a third world jungle on the island of Mindanao in the mountains above the port city of Cagayan de Oro those senses are on overload.

There's only a few possibilities in the fall of 1991 why any American, especially a 35- year old entrepreneur would be in these unnerving locals of the Philippines, but I'll get to that.

The topic of this essay is a moment that changed your life, and while just being there was quite life affirming, seeing as how I never flew till I was 34 and now was regularly taking business trips to Asia. There was a much more life altering experience ahead.

Thinking back, I remember leaving Hong Kong, a place that seemed very foreign and was suddenly thrust into an environment that was unlike anything I could have imagined. This was pre-internet, so unfamiliar destinations were not softened by Youtube videos and on-line travel blogs, suffice to say Dorothy, to me, this was not Kansas!

Arriving in Manila, at the airport I was accosted by dozens of people wanting to help me with luggage, transportation, directions and all for a fee. It was a sea of humanity desperate to earn from this arriving foreigner or any of the white faces they swarmed exiting the plane that day.

Twenty-four hours later I was boarding another aircraft for Mindanao, a roughly one-hour flight placed me on the largest most southern island in the archipelago.

The Cagayan De Oro airport was small and isolated, very much the opposite of Manila, although there were locals watching for the sparse landings and offering the same services as their northern brethren with similar fervor.

This was an open-air facility and the assault of heat and humidity was even more oppressive than Manila. I was met by my contact, another American, who was from Ohio and had a long history of doing business here. We loaded into his rather decrepit island car along with a guide and I was taken to check into the Pryce Plaza hotel, arguably the best lodging option in the area.

Several days later, I found myself and guide on a mountain road heading to the village of Malaybalay, where upon arrival we were to travel into the jungle toward a nameless array of island shanties.

I guess this is as good a point as any to explain my exotic whereabouts. It was to meet a group of rebels who wanted help getting gold out of the country. The gold was part of the trove reportedly left behind by the Japanese when they had to make a hasty retreat from the country during World War II.

Now the rebels I was meeting were just poor people who railed against the corruption of a current regime that lined their own pockets at the expense of their constituency. They had no connection to conventional terrorism. They just wanted to eat better.

As the current owner of a flagging furniture import business, I was introduced to this bizarre situation by my import contact, who was told of its existence by a worker at one of the factories we bought furniture from in Cebu.

Under normal circumstances I would have never even paid attention to such a ludicrous story, but we were in the throws of recession and my neophyte rattan furniture operation was taking a financial nose-dive. I thought if someone actually did have a pile of gold out there in the jungle somewhere, well I might as well be the one to help smuggle it out.

As part of my due diligence I needed to put eyes on the product and test it. The Philippines is notorious for scams involving gold, diamonds, precious metals and almost anything that can separate foolish foreigners from their cash.

After waiting in a small bodega for what seemed like many hours, our contact to the rebels finally arrived. I would come to realize that being on time has very little to do with an actual time in these parts. Transportation options and conditions in country were spotty at best, so everything was relative.

After exchanging a few awkward pleasantries, most lost in translation I'm sure, I was lead down a dirt road to one of the jungle shanties, where I was joined by six shoddily dressed men toting M-16s and gold bars wrapped in paper.

The procedure was explained a head of time, I would need to weigh the gold and be able to cut the bars in half and take core samples to insure that it was not a gold coated metal. I would give them a token amount of cash for the sample and then leave to have it tested. Once the results were confirmed, there would be other meetings and a plan would be set in motion to move and sell the gold. Not quite that simple, but you get the drift.

As I walked from that flimsy hut back toward the car, with gold samples in hand, observing the abstract poverty of my surroundings, I was given the gift of perspective. I was hit with how lucky I was to have the life, the resources and the country that I called home.

No matter what I faced in my life or business it was nothing compared to what these people and billions of poor around the world had to endure just to survive.

Since that day and for the 25 plus years since, I have lived with an overall sense of contentment without regard to any of the minor aggravations of my present circumstances. I realized that day that I'm one of the fortunate ones and that's something that should not ever be taken for granted.

And by the way, the gold samples tested 99.9 percent pure, but that's another story.

PRISCILLA RONDEAU

We grew up in a modest home, in a very quaint town in rural southern New Hampshire. My father, most often sullen and reclusive, made his living as a music teacher in a small town south of us in Massachusetts. My mother, always cheery and optimistic, worked in town in the administration office at our local high school. They shared a passion for antiques and their history. The drafty old antique home we lived in was evidence of that. It was on Main Street and dated back to the colonial days. With a spit and a half of land, we later considered it a "gentlemen's farm', reinforced by the fact we possessed numerous barnyard animals. This didn't necessarily make for happy neighbors, but there were always neighborly conversations. This idyllic existence was my norm; I knew no other. When contemplating this essay, I could cite several "watershed" moments that may qualify as life altering, such as when I lost a high school boyfriend in a car accident, or the day my son was born, but if I want to pinpoint the event that changed my life, abruptly and forever, I must relay a story, though while it originated long before I was born, smoldered to erupt and shatter life as I knew it.

Shortly after graduating college with a degree in Human Services, I had found a job in neighboring Vermont at a psychiatric hospital working with adolescents at a group home. Struggling to make ends meet, as is the norm for most newbies to the work force, it was always a treat to make the hour or so drive east for a weekend at my parents' home. Some special event was planned for the weekend, and I and my older siblings were going to be there. Unbeknownst to me, my life was about to change.

As my sister and I were helping with the preparations for the day, we started kidding with each other telling a story about someone who was being a nuisance. My sister suggested it would be best for all if we had just taped her mouth shut. I happened to glance at my Mom, and saw first a shadow cross her face and she turned, with now a terrified look, and left the kitchen. I dried my hands and set out after her, finding her on the back porch, sobbing. "What's wrong Mom? What happened?" Modestly composing herself, as best she could, she said "Priscilla I need to tell you something".

What followed changed me forever. She proceeded to tell me that shortly after birth, she and her twin brother we taken away from her "deemed unfit" mother.

Her mother earned this status, as she related, because the twin's father was not the man to whom she was married. This happenstance set Mom and her twin, my uncle, to spend the first nine years of their lives, always apart, and always bouncing around through a series of foster homes. They wouldn't meet until later in life. Although, and as if that weren't enough to give me pause, the real life altering shoe was yet to drop. My sister and I's joking reference to taping someone's mouth, had brought back with a rush, remembrance of abuse she had suffered at the hands of persons who had been trusted to foster her as a child. She continued on to share a few details of the abuse and which explained her abrupt reaction leaving the room earlier. While always aware of those events in her life, she hadn't thought about those awful times in a long time. My perspective on the pleasant and idyllic existence I had experienced until that time was forever altered by this new information, that my Mom had made it so, despite the shadows she carried deep in her psyche. Her cheery optimism, had not only ben an endearing feature, but transformed before me as a heroic trait. The more I turned it over in my head, the more courageous it seemed. Our quiet and unassuming mother never let show the pain she'd harbored, lest it cause discomfort to those she loved.

Over the next 37 years I would learn more and more about what horrors she had endured at a very young age. It was very difficult for her to share and very hard for me to hear. I've speculated why I was the one she told, after all I was the youngest of three siblings. Perhaps she saw in me someone who could handle and process the awfulness of her chronicle. She had once told me when I was younger it seemed it was to me that all my friends turned whenever they were in need of help or advice. Perhaps that's what initially drew me into the Health and Human Services field. I don't know. She would share something once or twice a year as her mood or the situation presented itself and the stories, while always brief, were never less shocking. She had been to many different homes, she wasn't even sure of the number, but I do remember a lot of stories in particular, coming back to two women, a mother and daughter, who had been very cruel to her.

Mom and I were always close and I found myself more and more amazed by her each and every day. Here she went through all these terrible things and she was the most optimistic person I'd ever met. She left the school administration job and followed her passion and started working for an antique dealer. Years later she would open her own Antique Shop.

My Mom had these different quotes some were her own some were from other people. Scarlet O'Hara: "I can't think about that right now. If I do, I'll go crazy". Most of the time she would shorten it to just "I'll think about that tomorrow". After a while I began to understand how that helped my Mom. Another was actually her motto for her business one that I use at my own business weekly:" a fast nickel is better than a slow dime". She was a wonderful business woman, well respected by her peers and customers. Having had the experiences she'd had, I've surmised it made her see clear through to what was really important. She was savvy but fair.

If my Mom had a flaw it was smoking. It was the "in" thing growing up and everyone did it. Looking back, it may have been a crutch, a coping mechanism. After all I'd heard, who's to fault her? It was a habit she or my Dad wouldn't ever break. She was diagnosed with lung cancer almost 5 years ago and died 9 months later, another life changing day. Yet, in the face of all this tragedy she was able to keep a childlike spirt. We spent our last lunch together out on a back patio of a restaurant in the NH lakes region. It was a beautiful warm fall afternoon and we were just enjoying each other's company. My Mom got up and started walking down by the lake. The next thing we know she was raising her arms and doing a little dance. My husband and I said to each other oh look she's dancing! We didn't think it out of character, she was given to moments of unbridled joy. Upon her return to the table we commented on her sweet dance on the lake's edge. She said oh darling I wasn't dancing I was avoiding stepping on the goose droppings! We laughed until we cried. She was a jewel and left us with that last precious gem.

RACHEL ARGO

It was Saturday 2/23/2008. I was going to the beach with 3 people from the church I attended to buy seafood for a fish fry. We stopped to eat and one of the other ladies wanted candy, so we ran into Wal-Mart to buy some for the road. We got about 45 minutes to an hour away. My phone rang. It was my daughter wanting to know why I wasn't answering the phone. I guess I was out of range. She said my mom was trying to get me. The hospital had called and William was there. I called the hospital and they wouldn't tell me anything except to get there as soon as possible. We turned around and headed back to Albemarle.

It seemed like a life time to get there, and then I went in. The doctor took us into a room and told us pretty much they had done all that they could. An ambulance had been called, and William was picked up. He was with a friend at another guy's house. The doctor said he was laying in his own vomit. I asked to see him.

I went in and he was connected to machines and tubes that were pumping his stomach. He never opened his eyes. My parents and I decided to have him taken to CMC Hospital in Concord. We followed the ambulance there and at least they were nicer and tried to do all they could. We each took time to talk to him and a tear ran down his face. My dad wiped the tear away twice. He never opened his eyes but was breathing with a machine at this time. They took him down to run some tests and then we waited. All this time I felt he would make it. You see, we had been through this before. The year prior when I got a call at 2:00am to go to the hospital, he had been in a wreck. He was thrown from the car. When I got there, his bone was sticking out through his arm and he had bitten his tongue almost completely off. I watched as they stitched his tongue back on. He was with the same friend that night as well. When I was pregnant with William, I was too small to have him. They had to take him emergency C section. He was stuck in my birth canal and had stopped breathing. He was born dead and when I came to from surgery, they told me he was born dead but got him breathing and rushed him to Charlotte.

I was so scared. I prayed so hard for God to let him live. My dad talked them into letting him take me to Charlotte in his van with a wheel chair. I was cut up and down not like they are now. They had to rush to save him. I'll never forget when we got there, he was in an incubator hooked to a machine and a tube pumping out his stomach. He had swallowed his first bowel movement. When they took him out and put him in my arms, I cried. He cued at me as if to say I'm ok. My dad was standing behind me and got to see it too. They called him Moose because he was such a big boy. He was 8 pounds, 2 ¼ inches and 20 inches long. They told me since his oxygen was cut off and he had 2 seizures that there could be something wrong. They could not tell me what time would tell.

As he grew, he was a happy, beautiful baby. He walked at 8 months and the only thing we found out later was that there was some hearing loss. I was told as he got a little older, he was ADD. I was always thankful that was all. In school, he struggled to fit in and had to take speech lessons from the hearing loss. I took him to one doctor that I was told was good with kids. He put him on Ritalin. He didn't like the way it made him feel and I did not like the affect it seemed to have on him. I took him off Ritalin and started trying to treat him with supplements and watching the additives in his foods. His grades came up and we finally had a teacher that between her and I working with him, he was doing better. He kept getting ear infections and his ear drums had burst 3 different times which wasn't helping with his hearing problem. As he got into high school, he started experimenting with drugs. The doctors later said that people like him try to treat themselves to feel comfortable and to fit in.

So this was always a fear of mine. They came to get us, and William was back in the room. We go up and pray over him while waiting to hear back from the tests. The doctor comes in and tells us there is no hope. His organs are shutting down. I remember crying and my daughter was behind me. She was my strength in the following days. I desperately needed to know more about his death. I went to the dispatcher that took the call. She gave me the tape but still to this day, I have not listened to it. She later called me and asked if she could give my phone number to the responders, and they would talk to me. I called them and at least I was told it was not how he was found. His fiend had tried CPR and called 911. When they arrived, he said they got him back breathing. After getting him to the hospital, he flat lined again and to their amazement, they got him back again. I will always believe he was waiting on us to get there. His friend and he had done a mixture of drugs with his prescriptions and pain pills. He went into cardiac arrest.

Though the years I have met many parents going through the same problem with their kids....Drugs...... I can relate to them and listen and understand. It has made me think how we all rush though life trying to do everything and not realize how short life can be. How precious the small things and moments are and we can never get them back. Not a day goes by that I do not miss his contagious laugh or his big teddy bear hugs. The only thing I can think to help is that at least God gave me 26 years. He really taught us all more than I ever realized. Like patience and trying to understand what someone is going through to make them react the way they do, the pain and struggle of everyday life is so hard and some just are not as strong as others. We should never judge what we don't understand. Addiction is a painful thing to them and to the ones that love them.

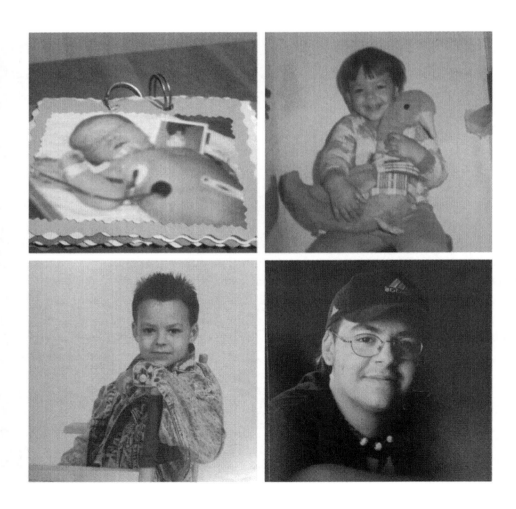

RALPH VALENTI

Jarid`s Pickerel

From his dad: God in heaven. You have taken someone who was so beautiful on the outside and amazingly more beautiful on the inside. Yes I am saying this because he is my son BUT I am also saying this because it is the truth. Please help him not to be in pain for missing his family. This will torture him beyond.

A background of who Jarid was is not easy, he was many things. An amazing athlete in many sports, holding two USA college male weightlifting records to this day. Somewhat of a legend in his high school, earning the nick name 'Tank". In basketball and football, people would chant, 'Tank','Tank'. Many of us have tank tattoos with his initials. The back of his arms had the tattoo 'trust' and 'loyalty'.

We now have a yearly scholarship fund in his honor, to the male and female senior athlete who exemplifies who Jarid was. Many athletic abilities matched with great character and much respect for teachers, coaches, school employees, players, and their parents alike. A very rare gift.

Yes, he was blessed with amazing looks and a great physique, but it really meant nothing to him. To him he would rather please others than himself. His huge bicep was not his largest muscle, it was his heart. His facebook page will explain much. What people said about him, is just inspiring.

You see Jarid would treat the janitor in his school with the same respect as the principal and charm them both equally. Sometimes he did it with a wink or his unforgettable smile, but mainly with genuine concern and care for you.

www.facebook.com/JaridValentiInMemory

A few quotes:

Nick, supervisor at East Greenbush, YMCA, thank you for the kind words yesterday about Jarid. You saw him grow up from a boy to a man there. You said this 'I am not sugar coating this, Jarid was the most amazingly kind and respectful person that I had ever met. You would not think that from a kid who was so physically gifted, but that is who he was."

Margo Walsh-perras He was always so appreciative with a strong smile and a hug that fell just short of breaking your bones.

Dan Sorino: Remembered being surprised how willing he was to help ANYONE out with ANYTHING, ANYTIME.

Nick Caruso I used to be Jarid's lifting partner at the Y. He used to be so impressed when I worked with 315 on the bench. A year later he blew me out of the water. Very strong kid. We were sad to hear he left us.

Keith Britt: Jarid... not a moment goes by that I don't think about what kind of person you were when we were younger, you never judged books by their covers and you were one of the most generous people I have ever met...still to this day!! You would give the shirt off your back for someone.....your missed everyday but I guess God needed another angel I LOVE YOU BROTHER!!

His dream to make our pasta sauce in all markets is becoming reality. The sauce is in many markets and the facebook page has over 13,000 fans!

www.facebook.com/VillaValentiSauce

Yes, a tribute to Jarid and his prom picture is on the label.

Now on to his miracle, Godwink, Jaridwink, we do not know.

A week after he passed away in my arms this happened. Myself, my daughter (his sister), Jarid's girlfriend, and her sister took a walk down to our beach in reflection.. Jarid and I fished here since he was a little boy. He loved catching a pickerel because they look so sleek and fierce.

As we walked onto the dock, we seen something shoot onto the beach at great speed. Looked like a torpedo, as it came in straight and perpendicular to the beach. Exactly at the beach's half way point.

To our amazement there was a huge pickerel. I went down and picked it up, we took pictures in disbelief. It was in perfect shape. Perhaps the largest I had ever seen. I proceeded to move it to the deeper water where it just stayed put for a minute and then swam off.

His girlfriend turned white and said that was for me! I always teased him `there are no fish in this lake'. Jarid always released his catch. His sister said that was for me! I was praying for a big sign.

 I did not say anything but to myself I knew. That weekend he passed, we were both shopping at Dick`s sporting goods for lures, we were to fish this week! I also knew pickerel was his favorite.

We were there for only a few minutes and yet this fish came to us at the exact halfway point of the beach. The circumference of the lake and at that point in time...too much to be a mere coincidence. Fresh water fish do not beach themselves and a pickerel does not let you pick it up.

Did Jarid do this for me? No, it looks like Jarid did this for all of us, true to who he was. How I miss you.

> Love you more and more,
> dad

SABRINA HOUSER

1996
I was 17 years old

At 17, I left home. For most this isn't an odd story because all I did was go away to college, like everyone else did. But for me, it was the first time in my life that I walked towards fear and not away from it, and that decision changed everything, because that was the start of the real me.

I grew up in a traditional Italian home and was one of the first females in our family to leave her parents' house before marriage. To make it worse, once I left, I never went back. College was always in the picture, but in my parent's mind, I was to commute to a local college and come home at night. I decided at a very young age I was not going to do that and when I was eleven, I started looking at other options for schools. By the time I was fourteen I was working to save for it and since the deal was if I went I away I was going to pay for it on my own, I started making smart financial choices about where to apply, where I could get the best education at the most reasonable price, and how I could make it the most affordable. I was young, I was completely on my own, I was alone, and I was terrified. If I failed, I would let myself down and I had no idea what my next steps would be.

My whole life, I have lived in fear. I was taught to fear our world, I was taught that I wasn't strong enough and I was taught that I couldn't do anything on my own, just me. And then I did. And I realized something very powerful about myself. I will always be afraid, but fear is what makes me move. Fear is what makes me work even harder. Fear is what keeps me up at night so I strive to put my demons to bed. I will never be confident. I will never be the person that walks into a room and everyone in it can feel my poise, my calm and my self-assurance, and that is now okay with me. I have realized you do not have to be confident to be successful; you just have to believe in your work and your effort. That moment could have hardened me forever, and for a little while it did. For many years I walked around with this chip on my shoulder that I needed to prove myself and my independence. I needed to prove to the whole world that all I need is me. Until I met someone that reminded me that real independence is being able to be on your own if you need to be, not because you are choosing to be. When I first met my husband, he softened me to the world again. He made me understand that I have all of the control I want over my life, if I let the anger go. He reminded me that this anger I was carrying was giving them the control over me and they were still impacting my decisions. To truly be me, I had to let all of that go and find out who I am without them. And so, I did. I no longer blame them for anything, I just love them for who they are and all they have given to me and to my family. I forever carry the good they instilled in me, like hard work and dedication and being true to your word and work. And although they don't even know it, nor was it their goal when raising me, they have majorly impacted who I am and I have come to truly believe that when I was little, they did the best they could with what they had.

But, my life is mine and who I bring into my world is my choice, my decisions. And years later, I came to realize that my life theme is walking through fear. It's where I find my strength and where I will forever be. The world is still a scary place for me, and my first instinct will always be to run away, but I won't let it paralyze me. At 30, I became a mom, at 31 I became the CEO of a nonprofit and a ran a marathon, at 33 we had our second child, at 34 I started a blog about my second chance at a childhood, at 36 I learned how to swim and competed in a triathlon, at 37 I became the proud recipient of a 40 Under 40 award and my next chapter is yet to be written. Yes, I continue to live in constant fear of trying and failing. But, it is that experience at 17 that taught me I will move toward fear and allow it to make me work a little harder for what I want to accomplish.

Sandra Homer

The second my life changed forever was on September 10, 2007 at 10:52 a.m. I was 8 months pregnant and at a scheduled ultrasound to check on Jayce's "movements". For about six weeks, I had noticed that something was wrong with my baby. Jayce was not moving like he used to. In fact, he was not moving at all. Still, I never actually thought the words; "we can't find a heartbeat" would be spoken to me. Even after all of my complaining, four emergency room visits, and multiple doctors telling me Jayce was fine, I never imagined my child would die. Then my fears became a reality when Jayce was born still at 38 weeks on September 11, 2007. He was full term, had blue eyes, curly hair and absolutely perfect in every way.

At the same time that I was beginning to mourn the death of my son…social media was born. Facebook exploded across the globe while my world collapsed around me. People from my past were requesting to be my "friend" over a social media platform, which allowed everyone to say what was on their mind and post pictures about their lives and loved ones. Sadly, Jayce was the only thing on my mind, and the only pictures I had of him were either ultrasound photos or his lifeless, bruised, and beautiful body. All I had to share and wanted to share with the world was my dead son. Facebook was literally like opening the door to your life and the whole world was on the outside waiting to walk in.

So, I began to share Jayce with the world.

I posted pictures of Jayce every day for six years, just like any mother would post pictures of their child. My status updates were about loss, death and, pain. At first, Facebook was a healthy and safe outlet for me to deal with my grief. As the months passed and my status updates and pictures remained the same, I was quickly awakened to the harsh reality of being judged and the insensitivity of people whom I thought were "friends."

"I am so sick of seeing your dead baby." As awful and disgusting as they are, those nine words changed my life forever, but for the better. How could anyone be sick of seeing my baby? Most importantly, why didn't that person just keep scrolling through his newsfeed and not comment at all? It was in that moment that I decided social media needed a safe place for people to grieve… "Heavensbook" was created on August 4, 2013.

HEAVENSBOOK by Sandra Homer
August 4, 2013
Months ago I had a crazy idea,
People posting pics and clicking "share"
Facebook is known throughout the world
Finally, on Thursday HEAVENSBOOK unfurled
My son died and my heart is still broken
Through this pain, my sweet Jayce has spoken:
"Mommy, please tell the world about ALL angels in heaven....
There are moments in time other than our 9/11"
Faces of angels, and memories coming alive,
Comments from loved ones who have survived
A digital place to share sorrow and disbelief.
People banding together providing relief
So here it is my sweet baby boy
It's a gathering of love, tears and joy
A place on earth called "heavens book"
A whisper from Jayce is all it took.

Within two weeks, there were 2000 members of Heavensbook and 500 people waiting to be accepted into the group. Heavensbook was unlike any other Facebook group because I created shout outs for every angel on their birthday and the date of passing (angelversary) through personalized photos tagging the member of the group.

After a year of Heavensbook shout outs I was approached by a childhood friend who was in the jewelry business and wanted to collaborate with me in designing a bracelet dedicated to angels. We designed a bracelet with my logo Heavensbook Angels engraved onto a circular halo charm. The bracelets were a hit and were selling at a fast pace. My friend had decided to move to Colorado to pursue an exciting opportunity and we parted ways. As far as business was concerned, I was left with hundreds of halo charms and the decision of whether or not to stay in the retail business on my own. Like divine intervention, I had a hair elastic in one hand and a charm in the other, the elastic fell from my hair and looped around the halo charm creating one side of a slide on bracelet. I quickly grabbed another elastic and a small key ring from my junk drawer and fastened the elastics together. The Halo Bracelet was created. My destiny as a jewelry designer creating affordable memorial jewelry was sealed.

The concept behind Heavensbook Angels jewelry is for the customer to design a one of a kind memorial piece to honor their Angel. No two items can be the same, as each one is sparked from memories shared between the customer and their Angel. Every piece of jewelry is handmade by myself and my mother in my basement. Together with keeping Angel's memories alive, Heavensbook Angels also has a Hope & Awareness jewelry line which focuses on raising awareness to the ailments which are a part of a loved one's life, or their memory. I have designed jewelry to raise awareness to cancer, heart disease, diabetes, MS, lupus, drug addiction, pregnancy loss, suicide, and of course, Stillbirth. Heavensbook Angels donates monetary percentages of profits to families in financial crisis due to medical bills as well as to foundations and non-profit organizations trying to raise money for a cause.

Today, The Halo Bracelet and The Forget Me Knot Bracelet are sold in over 125 retail locations including the popular gift store chain, The Paper Store. Online, my products are sold on The Grief Toolbox Marketplace, Amazon, Etsy, Open Sky, as well as my own retail website.

In addition, Heavensbook Angels has quickly spread across social media outlets ranging from the original Heavensbook group containing 4,500 members to the public Heavensbook Angels Facebook page. It has 38,000 likes and continues to rise in numbers each day. Between Facebook, Pinterest, Twitter, Etsy and Instagram, Heavensbook Angels now has a combined following of over 150,000 people in less than two years.

I hope my efforts from donations and raising awareness will help to ensure that not one Angel is ever forgotten and those of us who are mourning will always have an open space on Social Media to grieve freely...all in memory of my sweet baby Jayce.

Links:
Website www.heavensbookangels.com
Facebook: www.facebook.com/heavensbookangels
Facebook: www.facebook.com/HEAVENSBOOKHALOSHOP
Etsy: www.etsy.com/shop/HEAVENSBOOK
Pinterest: www.pinterest.com/Heavensbook11
Instagram: www.instagram.com/heavensbookangels
Twitter: www.twitter.com/HeavensbookA
The Paper Store: www.thepaperstore.com/search.html?q=heavensbook+angels
The Grief Toolbox: www.thegrieftoolbox.com

SARAH LOVELL

I would have to say that having had so many life altering events happen to me, the one that sticks out the most in my mind, would be the day I stopped putting drugs and alcohol in my body. It was November of 2004, and I was thirty three years old. I had been drinking and using drugs for eighteen years. I had been living in the streets, sleeping in basements, allowing myself to be destroyed in various ways by those who saw me as nothing but a plaything, a punching bag, or an object to help them get what they wanted. It didn't matter to me, as I already hated myself. I hated that I had been molested as a child, I hated that I had been gang raped at fifteen years old at a grown up party I had snuck out to. My self-loathing was so deep that I continued for years to punish myself and go along with that old story abusers always told me, "No one cares about you, so no one will believe anything you say."

By the time the only way I knew to make the pain stop began to turn on me, I was already its slave. I had become addicted to feeling numb. I filled my body with as much drugs and alcohol as I could, and despite the words I heard from the positive people in my life, it took me being what I like to call, "done" with that life. When the moment finally came, I was ready.

Lying in a hospital bed after having tried to destroy myself again and again, I felt that familiar urge to drink and get high. I looked at my wrists, they were wrapped in gauze. This wasn't the first time I had seen myself like this. Having run out of drugs and liquor, as soon as I started having any sort of memory or emotion without something in my system to buffer it, it was too much for me to handle mentally and emotionally, so I had lashed out at myself, cutting my beautiful skin. I needed just to feel something other than the pain that was spinning around in my mind and heart. While I looked down at myself, I started to pray. Begging God to save me from death was my last and only hope. At that moment, I was done. I didn't know that it was the moment. There had been moments of despair before that didn't stop me. I only knew it was over eventually because every day following that day, I continued to stay on track.

Now it was time to fly. I could feel it in my bones. There was no way I was going to sit still and just be. The need to do better was too great. Wanting to set an example for my daughters other than what they had seen from me in the past, I went back to school, opened my own business three months after graduating on the Dean's List, and started to work harder than I ever had at anything in my life. It was as if all of a sudden I realized that I had this insane drive to do more, to be more than I had the day, the week, the month, the year before.

Just so you know I began getting hit with devastating events having to do with my children. Through all of it, I never once considered getting high, or taking a drink. These things were so immensely painful, that I was often asked by friends how I was still breathing. My answer was always, "I just am." At times it seemed it was all I was doing, but it wasn't. I was helping other mothers and other girls. I was paving the way for myself and my children to have a better life. I just didn't know it at the time. I guess when you're building something, and have no blueprint, you don't realize the beauty of the thing you're creating. You just keep moving forward at your pace, no one else's.

These painful things that I've shared with you seem like another world, another time, and another person. Believe it or not, I carry some of that person still, especially the ability to scratch and claw my way toward each goal I set for myself. I never quit, because when you've been faced with things that are pure evil, and you've survived, it changes you. When you are one hundred percent sure that they can't do anything to you that already hasn't been done, then it kind of makes you hard to silence, hard to knock down, and most definitely hard to defeat. People begin to turn to you for guidance, for help, for support, and when you're ready, and strong enough, you give it.

I needed to get some of my pain out, so I wrote my memoir, "One Body". It's a quick read, but it packs a powerful message from me to anyone who may need it. There is something to be said for knowing someone else has been through what you're going through, and struggling with. Whether it's sexual abuse, domestic abuse, addiction issues, human trafficking, etc. I have experienced all of these things. I urge you to keep going, to find your strength within you. Sometimes it's so deep we don't know it's there. But I promise you it is, and when you find it, you will be a force to be reckoned with. You see, survivors

are special, we can withstand the worst, and end up the most beautiful when all is said and done.

So keep going, ask for help, and put your hand out to another who may be suffering. Keep moving forward.

www.facebook.com/Sarah-Lovell-747966425298892/
www.linkedin.com/in/sarah-lovell-3a3b9528

SHARON DONOVAN

I remember the day as if it was yesterday, June 8th 2005. There was nothing remarkable about that day, it was just another day in my miserable existence. I woke not sure where I was and then remembering, and thinking why? How did I get here and how do I get out of this?

I was in a co-workers apartment, in Taunton Ma., I don't even remember her or her boyfriend's name. What I do remember is that I was homeless, broke, and not sure what to do next. Kill myself or make that phone call.

I was sick, I had been sick for many years, sick of trying to make it through every day acting like I was OK. I couldn't keep it up any longer. I am an alcoholic.
I have two beautiful daughters that had decided that they did not want or need an alcoholic mother. They had put me out on the street, just like the garbage I had become. I had inflicted enough pain on them, they were done.

So, here I was, 48 years old, in a crack house apartment, with people I didn't know that had "taught" me how to smoke crack the night before. They scared the hell out of me… I took a look at the inch of Vodka I had left in a bottle and knew it was over. I had to make a decision.

I don't really know when I had crossed that line, the imaginary line between social drinking and alcoholic drinking, after my first divorce? Maybe? Second divorce, probably, definitely after my children grew up and moved out of the house and left me all alone… I could always find something or someone to blame…..it certainly wasn't me.

The phone call had to be made, as I poured that last inch of vodka into a glass, because only alcoholics drink out of the bottle of course, and drank it down. I knew deep in my soul that was my last drink, forever. I dialed the phone.
She wouldn't answer, three rings, four, and five … come on kid, and I really mean it this time. Finally, the voice of my daughter, 22 years old and the weight of the world on her shoulders, "Ma I told you to never call me." I begged her, please come and get me, take me to the courthouse, put me away….deep, please, do it now before I change my mind. She said I had 5 minutes to get ready she would be there to get me. If I wasn't out front, she was done.

I don't remember a lot from that day but I remember it all, if that makes any sense. They had me talk to a shrink. She agreed I needed help. They had me talk to a lawyer. He said they could put me in prison if there were no detox beds. I pleaded with them to find me a bed before the judge committed me. He said he wasn't supposed to but would see what he could do. Next thing I remember I was sitting in the courtroom waiting to be called, and the lawyer came out to where we were sitting and told me I have a bed... I looked at my girl and she said "there is your first miracle." And my journey began...

Detox was the worse, I had horrible seizures, the pain was unbearable at times but I refused most medication unless it helped with my seizures.

I didn't think I could ever live without alcohol. I just didn't know how. I was determined to beat this. I was going to be that one in thirty- eight that stays sober for at least a year.

After detox I waited for a bed in a halfway house, then on to a graduate house for a year. By this time my daughters were cautiously optimistic about my chances of staying sober.

I never lived in this city before, and found it to be a wonderful recovery city. Decided to take advantage of a program that provides apartments for people in recovery, rent free, for two years... I had a job and an apartment, but still had that safety net of being in a program and being tested every week.

Life started looking good, after 2 years I met my boyfriend. I wasn't looking but he was persistent. At that time he had 29 years of sobriety, and I felt safe.

For my two year anniversary of being sober, my daughters designed a special tattoo for me. It is a large butterfly that symbolizes renewal and redemption. Inside the butterfly's body is the head of a tiger, the most ferocious protector of her young, on either side are two butterflies, taking flight.... My daughters finally free of their mother's addiction and able to live their own lives.

June 8, 2015, my 10th sober anniversary, my daughters presented me with my medallion. I have a man that I love, a job that I love, and a new addiction... Riding my motorcycle, Life is good....

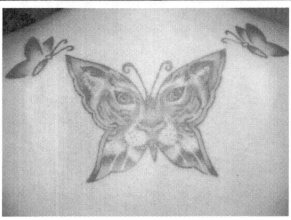

SUZANNE STRUSS

Gifts of Giving
Suzanne Struss and life changing experiences.
April, 13 2016, at age 64.

Born second into the Hurd family of 5 siblings in a small country town and blessed by hard working parents that revered loved ones first was the foundation of my upbringing. No matter how hard my parents worked or how late we may have been out on Saturday night, we all attended church to worship God. The specialness and encouragement I was given by my teachers and my family instilled confidence and high self-esteem.

Athletic opportunities were my focus and a passion. My teachers were my coaches and they cheered me on to participate at an elevated level in woman's gymnastics, swimming, and skiing.

I attended college for 2 years when my dad was taken in a tragic accident in front of my mom and the 3 youngest. I was the pillar for my siblings and mom. Leading them to the next step in such a tragedy seemed to be my role. Our family was changed forever. With life's promise before all of us I chose to be thankful and optimistic. It was then that I learned who benefited the most from my giving and that was me!

I taught and coached in a number of venues usually to children some of them cognitively challenged. I had part time retail jobs to fill in the money gaps along with a few home visits to help the elderly. I loved all of my jobs but felt the need to pursue a career. Real estate seemed to be the answer and I made a lucrative income and this is when I met my husband. We both were high level achieving goal getters until my long awaited son was born. It was in 1991, he is a real miracle. Our goals turned towards being parents that stayed present in his world and we lived out the same foundations as my upbringing. He was our only and along with his many friends we camped, den mothered cubs scouts, sailed, skied, volunteered at food pantries/community projects, and visited the elderly. Now at 24, he graduates from college in May. We still enjoy some of the same lifestyle together.

In 2005 our son began racing in a higher level through NHARA (New Hampshire

Alpine Racing Association) competing with USSA. His racing affiliation was at Mt Sunapee. My aging mom had developed a terminal disease and I remained the pillar with siblings to care for her in her last of living. She taught me so much about love, faith, thankfulness, and hope especially in her declining health. My husband and son were traveling every weekend to Mt Sunapee for race training. We really did not have the money to buy another pass for my husband, so he walked around the Sunapee base and into the A-framed NEHSA building. (New England Healing Sports Association) I visited over that season and was very fulfilled by what was being shared between all who entered NEHSA. Later that year my mom passed leaving a piece of herself while taking a piece of all of us and for that we are so thankful.

I returned the next winter season as a volunteer at NEHSA. I can go on and on describing the miracles that I see along with the other 400 volunteers there. I am now a PSIA certified Adaptive Ski Instructor (Professional Ski Instructors Association). I teach and mentor the differently abled population, disabled veteran athletes or the hope-to-be skiing athletes, and the children and all that is in between.

Quote: Nathan Fox, "Every day is like Christmas and every night is like Thanksgiving."

Suzanne Struss
Author
Suzanne Hurd Struss/Facebook

Affiliations
~Nominating committee for NEHSA
~Long-range planning committee for BWSC
~ Board of Governors for MHBC

Pictured are the many gifts I get from giving. Some are taken at the National Disabled Veterans Winter Sports Clinic and the NEHSA local veteran Winter Sports Clinic (WSC) while others are of the many that my affiliation with NEHSA serves.

David; USMC, PTSD, depression, homelessness, incarceration, transformed life through adaptive sports.
Kyle; ARMY, injured
Bill; Blind
Mikey; USAF, injured and an incomplete quadriplegic
Sarah; developmentally delayed
Erik; is nonverbal on the autism spectrum
Annalee; CP
Keegan; nonverbal autism spectrum

TIFFANY BEVERLIN

This story starts in a very unglamorous way, I was laying in my bed as I did every day during my dark, dismal divorce, after somehow mustering the strength to take my three children to school. When I say strength it's not a word you would normally associate with getting out of bed, but I assure you during those months, I was physically living on coffee and Cheeze. It's having dropped to 103lbs and being 5'8". I was malnourished, I was not sleeping, I was passing out from stress and anxiety, and I was seriously and deeply depressed. It took all the will power, strength, and love I had for my children to propel me to do anything at all. During these months of crippling sorrow, I was fortunate to have in my life one very patient, kind, supportive friend called Simon. Simon lived overseas, but he had been a friend of mine since we were 5 years old and had taken it upon himself to become my support system. He would call me regularly to ask how I am, check on me, and very sweetly and kindly encourage me to both eat and get out of bed. Neither of which he had been very successful at doing over that time frame. I would on every call give him a long itinerary of the devastation left from my divorce, how I had no money, no prospects, no skills, no hope, and no anything but the large list of wrongs that I had been dealt from my divorce. Looking back, I have no clue how he put up with me. I was negative, dramatic, and truly pathetic dissolving into tears constantly. I was almost 40. I had not worked out of the home for 12 years. Being a stay at home Mother and the idea of just magically reentering the workforce had become a ridiculous fantasy as I was told over and over again, I was unemployable.

On one such call with Simon something miraculous happened. Something that at the time I realized was big, but actually only in hindsight. I realized it was truly the second that was to forever change my life. Simon called, asked how I was, and I once again began with the long list of issues, problems, and miseries of my life. What made this day different was his reaction. He didn't say the usual, don't worry darling everything will get better and chin up pep talk. What he said was "For the love of God I cannot listen to this anymore, instead of making lists in your head every day of everything you can't change, why can't you get out bed, go downstairs and make a list of everything you can change. Do you have any idea how fortunate you are? Every day you have choices, options, and possibilities. So many people in this world do not." I was flabbergasted. I did briefly try and protest being the whiner I was when he continued, "every day you have the power to change the way you dress, your hair style, the gym you go to, your religion, who you date, your friends, and your career".

I got off that call, and I did as Simon said. I went downstairs and I wrote a list of everything I could change, and even better, I started making those changes and in the process, I began to realize the power of choice and of change. I stopped fighting it. I began to use change and my divorce as a giant spring board into better possibilities, amazing opportunities, and a happier life. In hindsight, I have come to the conclusion that if that one conversation hadn't happened, I would not have started my company, DreamsRecycled.com. I would not have begun making changes, shifting my focus into the things I could do as opposed to the things I can't do. I may not have been able to find a job, but I could start my own company. I may not have education in a tech industry, but I could research all the knowledge I needed online and teach myself. I wish someone had explained to me pre divorce that the entire process could have been so much less devastating and detrimental to me if I had focused all my thoughts, time, and effort on the future and what I had gained, instead of swimming for those years in the abyss of everything I had lost. My company aims to help other people do this, and founding my company is the single most important thing I have accomplished in my life. It helps millions of divorcees and will be left as a legacy for everyone globally to help them, and to spread the philosophy that divorce can truly be the happier ever after we all hope it will be, not the end of your life, only the start of a new exciting chapter. It has also shown me, in a glorious way, that I am capable of doing anything I set my mind to. Something that before

that conversation with Simon, I really believed in my core I was not. Now I literally wake up every day, jump out of bed, and have to reign in some of the thousands of opportunities I have discovered after changing my mind set, from what I can't do, to what I most certainly can do. This is an ultimate second of change, and also, I believe the most valuable one we can give ourselves daily. Belief in ourselves, and what we have the power to do. It is all entirely in how we view life and our attitude towards change.

Tiffany Beverlin
CEO/Founder DreamsRecycled.com

ULLA TIBBETTS

In the year of 1949 in Berlin-Germany where I was born, just before World War II ended, we were living in a house that had been damaged during the war. There was my mother, myself, and my stepfather. It was somewhat unlivable. I was born March 10, 1945.

After the war, Berlin was divided into 4 sectors…...American, British, French in the western part of Berlin and the fourth sector was the Soviets to the East. In 1946, if you wanted to travel from the Soviets, the allies created this Interzonen pass which we needed to travel from east to the western sectors. They created check points where you had to enter and prove who you were and why you needed to cross over. They would search you each time. My parents worked in the western sectors for that reason and had to endure these checkpoints. In 1948 when the Berlin Airlift began, the planes were landing every minute unloading and they repeated this for 12 months. The German people were very thankful. It brought their moral back and they could see a new beginning. My life would change in a second from here on out.

My stepfather had connections to the west and rumors were that it was going to be bad. The Soviets were planning something and my stepfather decided that we needed to escape. I was awakened one night in the early part and my mother spoke quietly to me. She said you have to be very silent and calm. We are going on a trip. No talking at all. We are going thru the back of the woods for a while. Don't be scared. I was 4 years old. She also said you can only take your Teddy Bear. We snuck out the house with just a few items like flashlights and some food for the way. We started thru the back of the woods, which later I was told was loaded with leftover mines from the war. Carefully we walked thru the woods. It seemed forever, not seeing much in front of the way and a bit foggy at times. After hours it seemed endless. We came upon a boarded old house where we rested. In a while there where two men coming towards us. I was so scared. They said a password to us. We knew they were helping us to go further with them. We arrived at dusk at a huge building like a school. It was divided with sections where blankets and beds awaited us. We had to give our info to the people. It was a refugee camp already filled with families.

My mother suddenly fell to the ground, kissed the floor, and started to pray. She thanked God for our safety and she turned to me and said, "We are safe now."

Little did I know the next night my parents would disappear in the middle of the night and again some stranger would be watching me. She told me, "Your mother will be back tomorrow and that's all you need to know." I found out later that they went back to bring some things for us, like bedding, clothes and my grandmother's Singer Sewing Machine. They took it apart and wrapped it in sheets and brought it across. The German people were determined. Finally I got to be with my parents. She said it's all over and we are save. We were issued passes and were given food, clothing, and money. We could stay there for three months but after that we had to find some work and a place to stay. We found a room for rent for one year and slept on air mattresses. My parents found jobs and I started pre- kindergarten. It was so amazing how my life just changed overnight. After a year, I even got to meet my half-brother who was captured after the war and now was free. We met after I was 13, and to this day have a relationship. It was such an exciting moment when we met for the first time. I also had a chance to reunite with my real father after many years not knowing him because of our escape. He was living in West Germany.

The Lesson I have learned is...Never take life or anything for that matter for granted. Be thankful for what you have, rich or poor, healthy or sick, it doesn't matter...you have to be proud who you are, and where you came from. It shaped my life so that I can be true to myself and others, helpful to others in many ways, don't need to be praised, just want to pay it forward, the way God has provided for me...We don't need much. We need to be kind and be there for each other, no matter who we are...

Dedication

The Second My Life Changed Forever is dedicated to everyone that has participated as writers in any one of my books. We all have a story to tell and we here at Unforgettable Faces and Stories are committed in creating a community of Storytellers.

Becky Coon
Debi Maynard
Donna LaFerriere
O'Neill
Eileen Truman
Mary Gibson Caron
Gail Gibson
Gail Thomas
Joan Ells
Karen Hubbard Arnold
Kaye Moynihan
Laura Sullivan
Laurie Arcuri
Patty Suprenant
Carolyn Doran
Cheryl Mazanec
Cheryl Frances Van Allen
Dan Doyon
Debbie Libby
Elizabeth
Heather Lutyen
Jacki Fish
Kate Kovac
Kathy Dunn
Katrina Heisler
Linda Ouellette
Mark Stoughton
Sam Doyon
Steve Smith
Terry Plaisted
Traci Knudtson
Tyler Libby
Alana Belliveau
Bernie Copeland
Debbie Reynolds

Ed Brewster
Emily Hodgman
Jennifer Gibbs
Kathy Penley
Kirsten Larsen Schultz
Lee Pecue
Lisa Fish
Lola Michelin
Lucy Kupish Delsarto
Marilyn Demont
Michael Day
Missy Covill
Sandy Fisher
Sharon Donovan
Stephanie Latinville
Terry Hyde
Ulla Tibbetts
Amy Fate
Andrew Attema
Ashley LaChance
Brenda Weeks
Cathryn Jae
Cheryl Lawyer
Christina Gardner
Donna Sears
Esther Hillner
Gail Robertson
Imelda Alvidrez
Jenn Schaaff
Kimberly Oiler
Randy Pierce
Regina and Andy Parker
Scott Mace
Shawn Vancura
Aisling Spofford

Alice Savasta
April McGinnis
Ashlynn Marracino
Carolyn Turner
Dianne Holland
Elizabeth Garrison
Cailyn Flynn
Emily-Anne Flynn
Allison Flynn
Fran Tunno
Jeanne Buesser
Jeanne Trombley
Karen Franco
Kimmy Lucas
Kris Sichmeller
Layne Case
Logan Beth Fisher
Mary Calhoun
Melody Turner Robinson
Mike Cassidy
Mischelle Miller
Nicolette Gardner
Pam Creighton-Hauschild
Pattie Bertoglio
Penny Robbins
Sheri Meekins
Teresa Wingler Alexander
Tim Burton
Tina Donbeck
Tracy Smith
Trudy Hancock Willis
Tyson Schmidt
Wanda Kezar
Yvonne Prince

Reviews

By Jenn Schaaff on September 16, 2014
Thank you Eileen for asking me to be a part of this series, sharing our story and photos, I am honored to share our story among so many other great stories of our Fur-babies. All of the stories in Pet Tales are all wonderful. My son enjoyed the stories we read together so much, I got him the e-book on his Kindle Fire so he could read them and see his "Chy girl" whenever he wanted. Thank you again & Be well!
~ Jenn Schaaff, CCMT
Pampered Paws K9 Massage
pamperedpawsmassage@gmail.com

By D. Diamant on August 31, 2015
Great stories of people and their furry companions. A great book to lose your self in. Friends of mine are featured and the stories are all real and worthy of sharing.

By William P. Fisher on September 2, 2014
Another great book by Eileen Doyon! For all the pet lovers out there this is one you need to read.

By Cathy Merrifield on October 2, 2014
Great book, make sure you have the tissues nearby! Randy Pierce is an inspiration, The Mighty Quinn lives on in many of us! Thank you for this wonderful book giving people an outlet to heal and share.

By Donna Sears on September 1, 2014
This book was amazing! Once I started reading the book I could not put it down. The stories are heartwarming. Some will make you laugh and others will make you cry but it truly is a book any pet lover would thoroughly enjoy! Eileen you are a caring and thoughtful person with such a huge heart-the fact that some of the proceeds of this book goes to a charity says it all. Thank you for letting us share our stories about our amazing pets! I can't wait to read your other books!

By William P. Fisher on November 2, 2015
Another awesome book by Eileen Doyon. Keep up the good work!

By Amazon Customer on November 12, 2015
Three words to describe the book: raw, real, and instructive. It is "raw" in the sense that Eileen allows the authors of the letters to speak for themselves. "Real" refers to the nature of the book: these are real people who left behind loved ones who are still reflecting on their losses. I believe that the book is "instructive" in multiple ways. It is instructive to those who will in the future experience similar losses. Simply reading the stories of others and how they processed the events will prepare those who have yet to walk the same path. To those who have already lost loved ones, the book can be an encouragement--they will be reminded that they are not alone in the struggle. Friends, family members, and counselors will gain insight into the inner world of the bereaved, and will thereby be able to support them more effectively.

By Beth on June 24, 2015
This is the sweetest book I have read. There are times I would love to talk to my husband. Never thought about writing him a letter. Until ...I read this book. I had the most wonderful feeling reading letters written to the love ones that crossed over to Heaven. People sat down and poured their heart out in the letters. I am thankful I had the chance to read this precious book. If you just lost a love one I suggest you purchase this book. Your heart will not carry a heavy burden. The letters will lift this burden. You cry because you are reading the best written letters..At times I felt a part of the family. This book is a keepsake..

By Jeanne Buesser on June 6, 2015
I wanted to thank Eileen Doyon for putting together this wonderful book. Letters To Heaven is a way of loved ones releasing untold thoughts or memories and healing their wounds. It makes the reader appreciate what life lessons were taught or special memories made. I highly recommend this book.

ByMimi Gallant on July 8, 2015
Beautiful compilation of heartfelt letters. Brought so many of my loved ones to mjnd. I would recommend this book for any/everyone who has lost someone dear to them. Beautiful, thank you Eileen

Amy Howard:
Just received the most beautiful gift and book-"Letters to Heaven" by Eileen Doyon. Each letter is pure and heartfelt inspiration. Each letter carries a theme

and life lesson of what is most important, what really matters, in our lives and hearts, now and to the end. All the letters are a testament to lasting love, special moments, and memories that will be treasured and cherished forever. This book is a source of comfort and inspiration for many as we all face or experience the love, loss, and pain of loosing a loved one. I think "Letters to Heaven" is a beautiful gift for those who are struggling with grief and who will find strength in reading these stories, comfort in knowing they are not alone in their feelings, and finding the courage and inspiration to share their own stories on paper. I will carry this book forward in my hospice work and encourage others to capture their thoughts, reflect on those memorable moments & memories, and send their Letters to Heaven. Thank you for a beautiful book and stories that need & deserve to be told.

By Ruth on August 26, 2014
Beautifully written stories from every day people! The author channeled her grief of losing her Father into a book and allowed others to do the same by sharing their stories and memories!! What an incredible concept!

By Ruth on August 26, 2014
Another amazing read by Eileen Doyon!! I'm looking forward to reading Best Friends and Pet Tales!!

Made in the USA
San Bernardino, CA
23 June 2016